Human Cloning

BIOMEDICAL ETHICS REVIEWS

Edited by

James M. Humber and Robert F. Almeder

BIOMEDICAL
ETHICS
REVIEWS

Human Cloning

Edited by

James M. Humber

and

Robert F. Almeder

Georgia State University, Atlanta, Georgia

Humana Press • Totowa, New Jersey

999 Riverview Drive, Suite 208
Totowa, NJ 07512

For additional copies, pricing for bulk purchases, and/or information about other Humana titles, contact Humana at the above address or at any of the following numbers: Tel.: 973-256-1699; Fax: 973-256-8341; e-mail: humana@humanapr.com, or visit our Website: http://humanapress.com

This publication is printed on acid-free paper. ∞

ANSI Z39.48-1984 (American National Standards Institute) Permanence of Paper for Printed Library Materials.

Cover design by Patricia F. Cleary.

ISBN 0-89603-565-4

Printed in the United States of America. 10 9 8 7 6 5 4 3 2 1

The Library of Congress has cataloged this serial title as follows:

Biomedical ethics reviews—1983– Totowa, NJ: Humana Press, c1982–
v.; 25 cm—(Contemporary issues in biomedicine, ethics, and society)
Annual.
Editors: James M. Humber and Robert F. Almeder.
ISSN 0742-1796 = Biomedical ethics reviews.
1. Medical ethics—Periodicals. I. Humber, James M. II. Almeder, Robert F.
III. Series.
[DNLM: Ethics, Medical—periodicals. W1 B615 (P)]
R724.B493 174'.2'05—dc19 84-640015
AACR2 MARC-S

Contents

Preface

The cloning of Dolly in 1997 was a shock to all. The day after Dolly's existence was made known to the world, President Clinton asked the National Bioethics Advisory Commission (NBAC) to assess the moral and legal issues involved in the use of cloning technology. When the Commission's report was released in June of 1997, one of its principle claims was that it would not be morally proper, under current conditions, to clone a human being. Undaunted by the Commission's report, at least one researcher, Dr. Seed, has announced his intention to clone a human. At present, the debate continues.

In this issue of *Biomedical Ethics Reviews*, seven highly respected authors examine the topic of human cloning from a variety of different perspectives. In the text the authors describe the procedure of somatic cell nuclear transfer and outline the history of cloning discourse. They analyze both the moral and religious arguments for and against human cloning, and in the process critically evaluate the recommendations of the NBAC. In addition, a number of authors discuss the effect that the creation of Dolly has had on our sense of self-identity and beliefs about the meaning of life.

This issue of *Biomedical Ethics Reviews* is the sixteenth annual volume in a series designed to review and update the literature on issues of central importance in bioethics today. We greatly hope our readers will find the present volume of *Biomedical Ethics Reviews* to be both enjoyable and informative, and that they will look forward with anticipation to the publication of next year's text.

James M. Humber
Robert F. Almeder

Contributors

George Annas • Boston University School of Public Health, Boston, MA

Jan Heller • Center for Ethics in Health Care, Atlanta, Georgia

Craig Klugman • University of Texas Medical Branch at Galveston, Texas

Thomas Murray • Case Western Reserve University, Cleveland, Ohio

Hans Tiefel • The College of William and Mary, Williamsburg, Virginia

Michael Tooley • University of Colorado at Boulder, Colorado

Richard Zaner • Vanderbilt University Medical Center, Nashville, Tennessee

Abstract

With the February 1997 announcement of the cloning of a sheep in Scotland, the ethics community found itself engaged in a century-old debate. Dolly, the cloned sheep, represents the first time that a mammal has been cloned from the differentiated cell of an adult. This chapter briefly traces the history of the technology of cloning as it relates to the social debate that has occurred around the topic. Starting with the publication of Mary Shelley's *Frankenstein*, five separate periods in the course of the debate are identified and outlined: (1) The fiction period (1818–1961); (2) frog cloning (1962–1977); (3) IVF and mammal cloning (1978–1993); (4) twinning (1993–1996); and (5) sheep renucleation from adult cells (1997–). From fiction, talk about cloning moved to issues of theology and philosophy on the meaning of life, parenthood, and marriage. In the 1990s, the conversation has dwelled more in issues of harm to the clone-child and on legal issues related to a clone. As the technology to clone a human has come closer to being a reality, the discourse has moved from the philosophical and theological to the legal and pragmatic. In the background of the whole debate looms a growing acceptance of the machine metaphor of life and of the body, which began with Leonardo da Vinci. This engineering concept of life means that parts are interchangeable, and one nucleus is as good as another. The conversation has moved forums as well: The first discussions occurred in books, but later talks moved to journals. In the latest period, however, debate has moved into the popular media, where pros and cons are dealt with as a public conversation, rather than as entertainment or an academic exercise. The last section of the article looks at the debate behind the National Bioethics Advisory Commission report on *Cloning Human Beings*.

Cloning, Historical Ethics, and NBAC

Craig M. Klugman
and Thomas H. Murray

One egg, one embryo, one adult—normality. But a bokanovskified egg will bud, will proliferate, will divide. From eight to ninety-six buds, and every embryo into a full-sized adult. Making ninety-six human beings where only one grew before. Progress.[1]

In 1932, Aldous Huxley presented his image of a *Brave New World*, in which all procreation was done artificially in large laboratories, and each cohort of children was cloned[2] from a single master embryo. He presented a frightening vision of a world in which classes of workers were engineered to be perfect for their place in society. Huxley's work was a warning to the world, a caution to carefully consider the implications of biotechnology for society at large.

Sixty-five years later, in 1997, the world awoke to newspaper headlines stating, "With Cloning of Sheep, the Ethical Ground Shifts,"[3] "Oregon Scientists Created Primates from Embryos not Adult Cells,"[4] and "10 Cloned Cows Soon to Be Born, Company Reports, Duplicating a Lamb Experiment."[5] The year 1998 began with the announcement that "Scientist Will Try To Clone Humans."[6]

The February 1997 announcement of sheep cloning was a page-one article. Public debate on cloning appeared in newspapers, on television, and on the internet. President Clinton instructed the National Bioethics Advisory Commission to prepare a report on the ethics and science of cloning, to guide the nation in developing policy concerning cloning. Open discussions in cyberspace and through media outlets, on whether to clone, indicated that Huxley's words were being taken to heart.

Six months later, in August, a page-10 *New York Times* story reported that calves, cloned from an adult cow, were soon to be born. These animals were cloned using a more efficient and reliable technique that shows that cloning is more fact than fiction. The public response was quiet; the article did not mention any ethical issues at all. In six months, concern over the caution heralded by Huxley gave way to the stifling yawn of reading old news.

Buried in the middle of the news section in the *Houston Chronicle* was an article announcing the birth of Molly and Polly, two lambs that were not only clones, but that were genetically engineered to produce a human blood-clotting protein. In the first week of 1998, what had only been a vague discussion became a concrete plan when an article on a scientist's intent to clone a human was published. That article appeared on page three.

The Machine Metaphor

The technologies that science now offers must be considered in the context of the history and culture of the society in which the technology is used. Alongside the scientific development of cloning over the last 60 years, one can trace an equally intriguing history of ethical and social commentary about those same techniques. These ideas and concepts challenge notions of the self, of the body, and of what it means to be human.

Several themes run throughout the cloning debate over the last century. One theme has been a change in the forum of the debate as communications technology has changed, and as bioethics has grown as a field. Discussion has moved from books to articles to the media, and now to cyberspace. Concern over cloning appears in fictional books and movies as well as in academic articles and list-servers. The cliché that science fiction has become science fact was never more true.

A second theme seen in the literature concerns that which makes even the conception of nuclear cloning possible: an increasingly mechanized view of humans as machines. The modern view of the body is as a machine, and that the body is composed of parts, and like machines, these parts are replaceable and interchangeable. If the muffler on a car does not work, one simply needs to replace it with another that has similar specifications. The same view applies to the body. If a liver fails, then it can be replaced with another one that has similar blood types and other matching factors. In some cases, as with pacemakers, insulin pumps, dialysis, and mechanical hearts, the replacement does not even need to be organic. Humans can now be equipped with artificial organs made from glass, steel, and plastic that are considered to be interchangeable with organic organs.

Such machine–human combinations were named cyborgs by Clymer and Kline in 1960, short for *cyb*ernetic *org*anism.[6a] "Bodies, then," Donna Haraway says, "are not born; they are made."[7] Haraway explains how society's conception of the body and of reproduction comes out of the concept of production and constructed beings. "An account of the biomedical, biotechnical body must start from the multiple molecular interfacings of genetics, nervous, endocrine, and immune systems."[8] The body is not viewed as a single entity that is whole in itself. Instead, science has reduced the body to component systems, organs, tissues, and cells. The health of the whole unit is seen as the proper functioning and interaction of the various parts. If one part ceases to work, medicine says that it can be replaced, and as long as the new part functions similarly, then the whole remains unchanged.

John Hoberman discusses his conception of the "technological image of man" in relation to athletes and sport. "The body of the athlete has become, quite literally, a laboratory specimen whose structure and potential can often be measured in precise quantitative terms."[9] The body, according to Hoberman, is an entity that can be manipulated through drugs and other techniques such as blood doping. "Sports science treats the human organism as though it were a machine, or as though it ought to be a machine."[10] Not just sport, but science as a whole tends to view the human body as a machine. Doctors can run tests on body fluids and tissues to determine if a body is operating at peak efficiency or at normal levels, in the same way that one checks the oil level in a car.

The modern biomedical body, then, is simply a highly mechanized machine. Such a construct is not a new vision of the human. In fact, Leonardo da Vinci viewed the body as a machine. He equated organs with parts, and believed that in mechanics and physics one could understand how the human body worked. For da Vinci, form determined function.[10a] This idea was also held and espoused by René Descartes.[10b] If the body is built of replaceable component parts, then all sorts of manipulations are possible, such as organ transplants or nuclear transplantation.

This growing acceptance of the body as machine has directed the changing debate in the literature. What ideas are of importance at any period of time depends upon one's view of the body as machine. For example, in the 1970s, concern over the meaning of family, especially in relation to clones, demonstrated a view of the human body as divinely inspired, one that could not be broken down into constituent parts. But when the debate later turned to questions of clone rights and of dangers to the clone, then the machine model of the body was not only accepted, but assumed.

Definitions

Before examining the literature of the cloning debate, one must note that the term "clone" has been used in many arenas, and with different meanings. Thus, a careful defining of terms is essential to any discussion of cloning. Cloning, in its modern usage, is loosely used to mean asexual reproduction of any kind, but the word used does have several specific meanings.[11] When scientists talk of cloning, they may mean asexual reproduction, as when cuttings are made of a plant, or when bacteria or other one-celled organisms procreate by splitting themselves in two. Other writers use cloning to refer to any type of genetic engineering.[12] Or, cloning can mean the replication of an identical copy, a photocopy if you will, of a gene, cell, or organism. Oskar Hertwig, in Germany in 1896, had yet another meaning for the word: parthenogenesis. Using seawater, Hertwig stimulated parthenogenesis in a sea urchin.[13]

When applied to humans, however, cloning usually carries one of two meanings. The first is popularly known as "twinning."[14] This is a process similar to what happens in utero when identical twins are formed by a fertilized egg splitting into two or more embryos. Twinning occurs in the laboratory when the buds, or cells, of an embryo are removed and allowed to develop, to produce twins of the original embryo. Cohen and Tomkin explain this as "embryo multiplication" or "blastomere separation."[15] This was the technological leap that was said to have taken place in 1993 when human embryo clones were created.[16] However, even this event was not cloning in the most contentious sense of the term.

Dolly represents the second definition of human cloning: "Taking the nucleus of a cell from the body of an adult and transferring it to an unfertilized egg, destroying the genome of the oocyte of the egg, and letting it develop."[17] Cloning is taking the diploid[18] nucleus from the differentiated cell of an adult organism, and placing the nucleus into an unfertilized egg from which the haploid native nucleus has been removed. Such a technique is also known as renucleation or nuclear cloning.

This idea was first stated by Hans Apermann, a Nobel Prize-winning zoologist, in 1938. Apermann is reported to have said: "This experiment might possibly show that even nuclei of differentiated cells can initiate normal development in the egg protoplasm."[19]

Dolly, the cloned sheep, whose existence was announced in February 1997, represented the first time that nuclear transplantation from an adult cell had been accomplished in a mammal. But Dolly was not the first cloned animal. In 1952, Briggs and King cloned a frog embryo by taking differentiated cells from a blastula and renucleating an egg.[20] The first organism born from nuclear cloning was announced in the literature in 1962. J. B. Gurdon took intestinal cells from a tadpole and renucleated an egg, from which a tadpole-clone was born.[21]

In 1975, the *American Journal of Obstetrics and Gynecology* reported that a scientist had removed the nucleus from a human egg, and replaced it with the nucleus of cells from adult testes.[22] This announcement was met with little fanfare. The birth of a mammal from cloning techniques, however, did not occur until 1981, when mice were born from renucleated eggs. The source of the nucleus for the eggs had been totipotent, embryonic cells.[23]

The mid-1980s saw rapid progress in mammalian cloning. In 1985, cattle twinning occurred,[24] and was quickly followed by nuclear cloning, or renucleation, using embryonic cells in sheep.[25] The following two years saw embryo renucleation in cattle[26] and rabbits.[27]

The Literature

In the period between Huxley's fictional vision of a cloned utopia and the newspaper printing of the fact of cloning, a detailed debate on the ethics of cloning has taken place. In step with the advancement of the technology of cloning have come heated discussions on whether society should allow cloning to be done. What is most noticeable is that during this long history of ethical literature, the issues and questions that are being dealt with in 1998 are the same ones that Huxley was concerned about in 1932.

The discussion of cloning can be divided into five historical periods. Each period reflects a new interest in cloning, usually preceded by a new advance in cloning technology or thought. An examination of any one of the periods would present a cross-section of the issues and concerns expressed throughout the whole history of cloning.

The periods are as follows:

I. Fiction
II. Joshua Lederberg and frog clones
III. Publication of *In His Image* and the birth of Louise Brown
IV. Human twinning
V. Sheep cloning

The discussion of each period is by no means exhaustive. The works selected represent a sample from each era, and are typically the ones that have been most influential upon the debate in later times.

During each phase, there is an expression of relief that the technology to clone humans does not yet exist. Even in 1993, with the announcement of human twinning, most writers indicated that adult mammalian renucleation was not going to be possible, and thereby put off discussion of that particular specter for another day. In the waning years of the twentieth century, what only recently was deemed impossible now looks to be around the next corner.

Phase I: Fiction

In this period, besides novels and short stories, there were publications on the science and ethics of cloning. Nonetheless, most of the phase I literature took the form of fictional stories offering "what if" scenarios. This period begins in 1818, with the release of Mary Shelley's *Frankenstein*. The tale cautions researchers not to "play God" just because they can. The power of controlling and creating life is an ominous one, and once a monster is created, there is no time for regrets. The time for thinking is before the experiment is done.

Following Huxley's 1932 *Brave New World*, science fiction next took up the banner of cloning with Charles Eric Maine's

World Without Men (1958) and Poul Anderson's *Virgin Planet* (1959).

In 1947, C. S. Lewis gave a lecture entitled "The Abolition of Man," which was later published as a book. This essay represents the earliest public, nonfiction commentary on cloning. Lewis was concerned that the values of one generation could irrevocably change the destiny of future generations—that the vision and goals of the parents may be the nightmares and obstacles of the children and grandchildren. "One dominant age...which resists all previous ages most successfully and dominates all subsequent ages most irresistibly,"[28] he wrote.

This phase represents a period of possibility. The literature explored human cloning by way of biological and social change. Such works could warn of the dangers of taking technology to extremes. This social commentary could be expressed as fiction without worry of true human cloning being possible in the near future. Both the positive and negative potentials of cloning could be examined in a free and unstructured manner. The works were highly speculative and carried religious themes, examining the relationship between humans and the divine. Most of these works can be viewed as warnings on the dangers of cloning, not as utopian blueprints.

Phase II: Joshua Lederberg and Frog Clones

The second phase saw a continuation of the fiction tradition. In 1973, Nancy Freedman published *Joshua, Son of None*. Then, in 1976, Ben Bova released *Multiple Man*; and Ira Levin's tale of cloning 96 Adolph Hitlers, *The Boys From Brazil*, reached the bookstores. In the early 1970s, Woody Allen's comedy movie, *Sleeper*, used the idea of cloning a dictator from his nose as a central element of the plot.

However, beginning in 1962, when Gurdon cloned a frog for the first time, the literature took on a decidedly more academic tone. This is one of the longer phases, extending from approximately 1962 through 1977. Much debate in academic and legislative circles took place, and treatises on the issues of genetic engineering, eugenics, and shaping human destiny were published.

The cloning discourse took on a new tone with an article written by Dr. Joshua Lederberg in 1966.[29] This may not have been the first cloning article, but it certainly has been one of the most influential—a catalyst that is still mentioned in contemporary dialogues. In "Experimental Genetics and Human Evolution," Lederberg speculated that there may be many applications of cloning. He examined the notion of positive eugenics through genetic engineering (i.e., algeny) and cloning. Lederberg pointed out that he was making "comments," not "advocacy,"[30] for these positions. Like Huxley, he painted a picture and examined the implications; he did not intend to predict the future. However, it seems that he may have inadvertently done so.

> If a superior individual (and presumably genotype) is identified, why not copy it directly, rather than suffer all the risks of recombinational disruption, including those of sex. The same solace is accorded the carrier of genetic disease: why not be sure of an exact copy of yourself rather than risk a homozygous segregant. [31]

In one paragraph, Lederberg laid out much of the debate over cloning for the next 30 years. His eugenics argument is cited by both advocates of cloning and opponents to it. Lederberg said that cloning is a way to increase the rate of evolutionary change in humans. He expressed the idea, popular at the time, that modern medicine and technology had allowed those who were evolutionarily unfit to survive and reproduce. Modern life had removed selective pressure for Darwinian evolution, thus "weakening the species."

If large numbers of individuals were cloned, they might be perfectly adapted to a particular environment, Lederberg said. He added, "We would at least enjoy being able to observe the experiment of discovering whether a second Einstein would outdo the first one."[32] But if that environment should change, the clones may be unable to adapt, and with a limited gene pool, that could spell the end of the human species. For example, say a blight struck only people with five fingers, but allowed those with six to survive. If there were only ten genetically distinct clone lines, none of them might have the six-finger gene. Thus, the decrease in genetic diversity would lead to the extinction of humanity. Lederberg suggested using both cloning and sexual reproduction to overcome this drawback.

Another danger, according to Lederberg, was that the technology could be used as a form of genocide, to weed out those found to be undesirable. He also acknowledged that cloning could be seen as a form of narcissism for those who could afford the technology.

Lederberg saw the need to look at legal issues, the status of clones as chimeras and "subhumans," the use of clones as organ donors, and what to do with experimental mishaps. The last two pages of his article seem to predict the concerns of the fourth phase, in which ethicists are concerned about the place of clones in society, and about their legal standing. The concern over mishaps is a key point in Paul Ramsey's publications in the third phase. It is also a key worry today.

What Huxley tried to do in fiction, which was to force people to examine the place of technology in society, Lederberg tried to do within the academy. Ethical discussions have been playing catch-up to scientific realities even with the warnings of these authors. The flurry of discussion that took place in the late 1960s and early 1970s showed that a few thinkers, mostly theologians, were trying to anticipate where science and technology might lead society.

Paul Ramsey, in *The Fabricated Man*, expressed his reservations about cloning. He was concerned with Lederberg's scenarios and assumed that Lederberg was advocating cloning and eugenics. Ramsey's rebuttals and concerns have set the tone and foundation for much of the later debates on cloning. However, all of his arguments in favor of cloning, and many of his arguments against it, come directly from Lederberg's article. What differs between the two are the reasons that Ramsey offers: Lederberg rests his case on secular thought, Ramsey's stance is avowedly theological.

Ramsey conceded that there might be some benefits to cloning. Among those he listed were to

1. copy a desired individual;[33]
2. become a biological parent without the risk of passing on a recessive disease to an offspring if both parents are carriers, (e.g., sickle cell or Tay-Sachs);
3. control the biological sex of offspring;
4. create beings with interchangeable parts (i.e., compatible organ transplants); and
5. achieve that special cohesion and communication that twins seem to have.

Although he recognized these interests in cloning, Ramsey was very much against the technology. Genetic engineering, and cloning in particular, he felt meant "playing God." By using scientific power to control and shape humans, people become less than human. He cited several reasons as to why cloning should not be done.

1. Loss of genetic variability.
2. Problems with the ethics of experimenting on humans.
3. What to do with "mishaps?" He defines a mishap as an embryo that may be damaged or malformed in the test tube, or an embryo that might be implanted into a woman, but be grossly malformed, so that it would have to be aborted. In both cases, his concern was with the wanton destruction of these laboratory creations. Such considerations stem from his views on the status of the embryo as a potential human being. He also expressed belief in the sanctity of all human life.

The next two concerns demonstrate Ramsey's originality. Here he does more than just argue against Lederberg.

4. What is the nature of human parenthood? Ramsey was concerned that cloning disregards the covenants of marriage and parenthood. In parenting and procreation—notice that cloning is reproduction to Ramsey, not procreation—he sees an expression of the love of the marriage partners, and of the love between God and humans. "In this [procreation] there is a trace of the original mystery by which God created the world because of his love."[34]

   For Ramsey, covenants are representative of the love, not only of families, but also of God. This love is manifest in the act of procreation, an act which takes place between a man, a woman, and God. In the context of procreating, "the two are made one." That is, the man and the woman become of "one flesh," which manifests itself in the flesh of their child. Cloning, according to Ramsey, denies this central meaning. "If cloning men had no other consequence, this alone would be sufficient to fault it."[35] In other words, Ramsey felt that the covenants of marriage, family, and parenthood might be lost, and that would mean also losing the love of God.

   The term "reproduction" is a focus on production and mechanical means of creation, reducing the human body to the status of machine. It is against this conception that Ramsey argues. Thus, he sees value in using the term "procreation," which places humans in the realm of nature, and treats the human as a whole entity, rather than just as the sum of all its parts. A reductionist and mechanical view of the body also disrupts traditional notions of personhood. If the body can be separated into replaceable parts, then so can the person. The machine metaphor also has the effect of separating the individual from the body, as if the personality could be transplanted to reside in any suitable corporeal shell. For Ramsey, such an action is a denial of one's humanity, and also a denial of God.

5. Loss of individuality and personhood. "The entire rationalization of procreation—its replacement by replication—can only mean the abolition of man's embodied personhood."[36] The body, the soul, and their combination make each individual unique, according to Ramsey. Genetic technologies threaten to change the body and a person's individuality—to obliterate it. With multiple copies of each person wandering around, that uniqueness is diminished more, and becomes banal.

In true nuclear cloning, one creates life in a way that would not happen in nature.[37] The donor-parent and the clone are faced with a violation of the sense of individuality, a loss of genetic uniqueness. Even in twinning, the genome that is created in the original embryo, before it is twinned, whether in a laboratory or naturally in the uterus, is unique in nature. The genome in a clone, however, even if its phenotype is different, and even if its psychology and personality are different, still does not have a unique gene set. The genome in the clone's original first-cell stage is probably slightly different than the genome that was in the donor-parent's first cell, but that difference is caused by aging and environmental damage, rather than by the creation of a new genome that has never existed before—a unique organism. Cloning threatens individual uniqueness. Whether that is a social and cultural value, though, is something that needs to be debated. Perhaps society will decide that conformity and similarity are more desirable.

Ramsey's point on parenthood losing its meaning is pertinent to any discussion that redefines reproductive roles. Besides the loss of the covenant concept of parenthood, the titles of parent, mother, and father lose meaning. After all, "[Is] a mother a mother to the clone of her husband? Is the father, the father or a brother to his infant clone?"[38] One must consider the bizarre family relations that could occur. A woman could give birth to the clone of her father, her husband, or even herself. Would such progeny be her child, or in the case of giving birth to her own clone, her twin? A pedigree chart for such a cloned family would look like a tangled web.

Another point of contention is over how one defines who the parent is to a clone. Realistically, a clone could have up to seven parents: (1) the donor-parent; (2) the donor-parent's genetic mother; (3) the donor-parent's genetic father; (4) the egg donor; (5) the surrogate; (6) the adoptive or rearing mother; and (7) the adoptive or rearing father. And if the clone is the progeny of another clone, then the list of possible parents becomes even longer and more convoluted: Thus the necessity for defining, legally, who the parent is where a clone is concerned. Who has responsibility for the upbringing and education of the clone? Or is the clone brought up by a community of parents, rather than by specific individuals?

In 1970, Alvin Toffler published *Future Shock*, an attempt to make people think about the future possibilities that technology creates. In this book, Toffler states that the world is changing faster than some people can handle. He proposes using the potentialities that are seen in the future as a tool to examine the ideals and values of the present. By deciding on a vision of the future and what values are important, society can direct what future it wants. He makes brief mention of the question of cloning, looking at it as a consequentialist would, as a means to an end. "Cloning would, among other things, provide us with solid empirical evidence to help us resolve, once and for all, the ancient controversy over 'nature *vs.* nurture' or 'heredity *vs.* environment.'"[39] As a journalist, Toffler never states whether he approves or disapproves of cloning, but advises caution nonetheless.

Rabbi Azriel Rosenfeld, in 1972, offered his concerns that cloning and genetic engineering would destroy family relationships and connections. Certainly, he contended, concepts of parent and child, as well as relationships between siblings would need to be altered. A person could legally, under halachic (Jewish) law, be born without a father. He concludes that cloning can be permitted, because reproduction through such a technology would not be considered a sex act, and therefore, not forbidden under Jewish law.[40] Although not necessarily a boon to society, he would permit cloning, because he can find no legal basis for limiting or prohibiting it.

Willard Gaylin, then president of what would become the Hastings Center, wrote an article for *The New York Times Magazine* in 1972. He believed that some good could come from cloning techniques. One application would be saving endangered species by allowing scientists to increase the population. Whether this would be done through twinning or nuclear cloning, Gaylin did not specify. Today, one could speculate that cloning may bring back extinct animals, as in *Jurassic Park.*

One of Gaylin's fears is that genetic engineering might stop evolution and weaken the human gene pool. Of course, the argument could also be made that medicine does this by healing the sick and letting them procreate, instead of removing their genes from the evolutionary pool.

Like Ramsey, Gaylin said that artificial reproduction, such as cloning, removes the creation of life from the bonds of marital love and the sexual act. Gaylin also questioned what cloning might do to conceptions of the sanctity of life. If cloning were commonplace, people might become accustomed to mishaps and damaged children. Being blunted to such side effects of genetic engineering concerned Gaylin.

> The tragic irony is not that Mary Shelley's "fantasy" once again has a relevance. The tragedy is that it is no longer a fantasy—and that in its realization we no longer identify with Dr. Frankenstein but with his monster."[41]

A proponent of cloning, Joseph Fletcher, in *The Ethics of Gene Control* argued that not only should cloning be pursued, but that it is protected by law and tradition. He used freedom as a moral principle and saw reproduction as a right, as long as it is done by consenting adults. A utilitarian, Fletcher asked if cloning maximizes happiness. He answered yes, that biological relationships in a family are not important. Families are based on social obligations, and it is the social aspect of a family that counts, in his opinion.[42]

Leon Eisenberg, writing in the *Journal of Medicine and Philosophy*, expressed concern over the loss of genetic diversity that could result from cloning on a large scale. Although the gene pool might shrink, he did not think that individuality would be constrained at all. He cites evidence that postnatal development of the brain depends on environmental stimulation. Since the environment, and therefore the stimuli, of the clone would differ from that of the donor-parent—simply through the effect of being members of different generations—the clone would have a different brain than the donor-parent.

In general, Eisenberg supported cloning because attempts to stop it, he said, would be an ineffective show of force by the government. He believed that no technology was innately good or bad. Whether a technology is a good or an evil depends on how it is used. The mere existence of the technology itself is neutral. He would rather not place the power in the hands of the legislature.

> It is not knowledge but ignorance that assures misery. It is not science but its employment for inhuman purposes that threatens our survival. The fundamental ethical questions of science are political questions: who shall control its products? For what purposes shall they be employed?[43]

Eisenberg saw the debate not as one of whether cloning technology should be pursued, but as a question of politics and control. Each should be considered independently: Should there be cloning; and who should control it. However, since science exists in a political and cultural context, what science does and how science does it has a big impact on the society, and on the world at large.

The year 1977 represents the end of phase II of the ethical literature. *Who Should Play God?*, a book by Ted Howard and Jeremy Rifkin, was published. Rifkin is very much against certain technologies, especially science that has the potential for changing life and humanity so drastically. He argued that no genetic engineering, including cloning, should be permitted.[44]

On the other side, the writer Vance Packard called not for a ban on cloning, but for a new way of thinking about life and ethics in his book, *The People Shapers*. Ethics needs to incorporate ideas of cloning, he said. "A new set of human ethics would seem to be required."[45] Packard's response fits neatly with Rifkin's 1983 criticism of ethics—that ethics seems to sanction, not question technology.

Phase III: Publication of In His Image *and Birth of Louise Brown*

Phase III differs remarkably from the preceding eras. For the first time, manipulation of human embryos and laboratory-produced children were a reality. Fiction had become fact. Two events were the impetus for this new round of ethics debates. Louise Brown was the scientific proof that IVF techniques worked—such tools would be necessary for cloning. The second was the startling publication of *In His Image: The Cloning of A Man*,[46] a book by the journalist David Rorvik.

Rorvik's book tells the story of a millionaire who finances a scientist, outside of the United States, to create a clone of the wealthy patron. At the end of the book, the procedure has been successful, and the surrogate mother has gone to the United States to give birth to the clone. This book echoes Lederberg's suggestion that cloning might be a form of narcissism. It also seemed to exemplify his warning that science will just go forward without examining its implications on society, and that such technological leaps may take society by surprise.

Scientists quickly declared Rorvik's book a hoax.[47] A Congressional subcommittee looked into the issues surrounding cloning. People wanted to know if indeed a human had been cloned. Rorvik failed to appear when called before the subcommittee, and would not release any confirming information.[48] The book, it was decided, was a sham and little discussion on cloning actually took place. However, Rorvik never recanted the claims in his book. The final congressional report stated that renucleation in humans was neither feasible nor desirable.[49]

Rorvik's tale of human cloning, along with Louise Brown's birth, brought concerns about cloning to the forefront. Compared to the other phases, this was a quieter era as far as cloning literature is concerned. Many of the voices in the discussion are still theological, but a shift toward more secular and legal thinkers occured.

Richard McCormick added his voice to the cloning debate. He wrote that cloning and genetic technology force one to question what it is to be human. This, he thought, was a negative aspect of genetic engineering, not just cloning.[50] McCormick's concern is one of the oldest themes in cloning ethics, beginning with Huxley, and is expressed most eloquently by Ramsey.

In 1979, Fred Rosner mentions that Jewish laws are said to apply only to those things that can be seen with the eye, a concept that would seem to sanction cloning. Still, he does not believe that this gives blanket consent. His misgivings have to do with the family and the meaning of procreation—a very common theme in theological writings. One might say that this issue has been the paramount point of contention in religious circles, though by no means the only concern. "There are three partners in the creation of a human being: the mother, the father, and G'd. Cloning of man negates identifiable parenthood and would thus seem objectionable to Judaism."[51] Judaism and Christianity, or at least Rosner and Ramsey, would seem to be in agreement on this point.

The early 1980s were fairly quiet. The mid-1980s, however, began a period of massive development in the technology of cloning. Just prior to embryonic twinning and cloning in mammals, a presidential commission's report, *Splicing Life: The Social and Ethical Issues of Genetic Engineering* declared that genetic engineering is a good that should be pursued, but must be used responsibly. As far as cloning was concerned, the report merely said that human cloning was not considered a realistic possibility, so it should not be considered in debate.[52] Considering that only a decade later human twinning was performed, such a brushoff may have been shortsighted.

Or, perhaps cloning isn't a problem. In *The Gene Business*, Edward Yoxen says that cloning is really no big deal. Considering its costs, the technology would only be available to the wealthy few who could afford it. Cloning, then, would never become a major force in society.[53] One could also argue that the price means the technology would only be available to a privileged few. This could lead to a division in society between the clones and the "sexuals." Such a distinction could mean power being driven into the hands of one group, and discrimination being forced upon the other. Thus, cloning could become the fashionable way to reproduce, something to be desired and worked for. Families might save money for years to achieve this dream. To be born from a sexual act could become shameful. Such a scenario is played out for genetic engineering in the movie *GATTACA,* but not cloning per se. Although Yoxen believes that price relieves concern about the mass use of the technology, that same fact could mean cloning becomes a political and economic tool of oppression.

Jeremy Rifkin, in *Algeny*, 1983, warned against using genetic engineering technology and cloning. Among his fears were that eugenics would be employed the way the Nazis used it, or the way Americans used the concept to sterilize the mentally retarded. Rifkin said that he does not trust ethics to control use of technology, because ethics tends to bless all scientific and technological progress. Instead of cautioning or regulating, ethics tends to push such research ahead.[54] Although ethics tends to question new technologies, often it is in the context of how to use them responsibly, of forming commissions to advise the public and politicians, and of discussing how further research in the area should be done. Rarely, Rifkin asserts, do the voices against using the technology get heard, and almost never are those opinions adopted.

Algeny emphasized that society seems to follow the machine metaphor. One might consider the earlier argument about the terms "reproduction" and "procreation" when considering the meaning of the machine metaphor in science and human life. The machine metaphor, as a way of interpreting the human body, has increasingly dominated social and scientific thought in the twentieth century. Human parts, whether organs, genes, or nuclei, are seen as interchangeable. One nucleus can be exchanged for another, and both are considered equivalent. The whole, in this image, is not greater than the sum of its parts. The result is a dehumanization of people and an embodiment of the machine into each person's view of him or herself. The pursuit of modern biotechnology has only become possible with this view of the human body, in which people are merely means to an end. Huxley's horrifying vision seems especially poignant in this light.

The switch in tone, from questioning the meaning of life and what it is to be human to a question of how to incorporate clones into society, indicates a change in the discourse. Theological discussions become overwhelmed by the voices of legal thinkers, and other secularists readily accept the machine metaphor without questioning its application, or even its appropriateness as a framework in which to discuss medicine and human life.

In 1984, Peter Singer and Deane Wells published *Making Babies*. Singer and Wells believed that cloning could be restricted, based on the possibility of harm to the offspring (the clone) from using unproven technologies. But their decision to allow such limitations was not easily reached:

> We believe that the state can be justified in interfering with the decisions to reproduce, either in order to control population growth or to prevent practices that might disadvantage the children born. But we also believe that the state should interfere only in the most extreme cases...Cloning does not appear to be so extreme a case...
>
> The risk of something going drastically wrong is, at present, a sufficient reason for the state to prevent individuals from

> cloning themselves. Should it one day be shown that this can be done without risk, we would reluctantly concede that while the government should not assist in the process perhaps it should not prohibit it either.[55]

If cloning is permitted, then Singer and Wells suggested limiting the number of clones that a person could have to one. The restriction would prevent problems, such as a decrease in social and genetic diversity. If there were no limits, then it might be possible to have a hundred clones of a single person running around. Such "limited editions"[56] might be considered valuable resources. Placing a Mahatma Ghandi in the capital of every country might drastically affect international politics—assuming what is manifestly false, that a clone is indeed a photocopy.

A mass of clones, however, could decrease the value of the original. A clone clan also opens the donor-parent to being the victim of fraud by clones impersonating him or her. Bill Gates clone #95 could walk into a bank, pretend to be the chairman of Microsoft, and withdraw a great deal of money. Overnight, the real Bill Gates could become a very poor man.

Echoing back to Ramsey and concepts of personhood, Leon Kass believed that cloning inherently injures an individual. His concern was that cloning would decrease the dignity and the worth of each person.[57] One could take his argument further. Say that there are 10 clones of Julia Roberts. If a producer or director is not happy with the donor-parent Julia Roberts, why not just get one of her clones? Perhaps a clone will be hired right from the beginning, because he or she will work for less money. Real wages could drop considerably, since there would always be an alternative. This may, though, lead to an underclass of poorly paid clones. The value in dollars and in dignity are decreased by having multiple copies of a person. One might call this the cheapening-of-life argument. Such a contention only works when based on physical appearance, since temperament and character are likely to be different in each and every clone.

Clones would probably have psychological pressures to live up to parental expectations. In other words, parents may expect their clones to be just like the donor-parent. A clone of Mother Theresa may have a difficult time growing up in a home that expected a photocopy clone of the original, especially if the clone's interests tended toward being an agnostic stockbroker.

Other words of caution were expressed by the Council of Churches. Finding no legitimate reason for cloning, the council was appalled by the lack of legislation barring such research. "We know of no existing laws or regulations to prohibit such experiments. We know of no goal legitimate enough to warrant such radical experimentation."[58]

Even if the United States were to consider banning human cloning altogether, as the member countries of the Council of Europe, as well as the state of California, have done, Ira Carmen, in 1985, claimed that the Constitution forbids the federal government from doing so. Carmen's argument was that choice of research topic is a protected form of self expression that falls under the First Amendment.[58a]

Carmen goes further and says that genetic engineering and cloning are protected under the concept of procreative liberty (a concept that Robertson has discussed often). The right to procreate, even clone, he claims, is protected under the right to privacy and the tenets of *Roe v. Wade* to control one's own body.[59] Of course, *Roe v. Wade* does state that there are circumstances when the state has a right to protect the fetus over the wishes, but not the health, of the mother. For example, the Court has restricted access to abortion in the third trimester of pregnancy. If a woman generally has the right to control her own body, then that same right allows one to clone his or her genome, as long as the donor-parent is consenting. That does not give one the positive right to have a surrogate to gestate the fetus, or to have a laboratory create the clone, just as federal funds cannot be used to pay for a woman's abortion. She can have the procedure, but the state will do nothing to help her get it. This, then, is a negative right. The same sort of rights, Carmen claims, should apply to cloning rights.

One of the few discussions of cloning from 1986 to 1992 is a piece of fiction: Fay Weldon's *The Cloning of Joanna May* in 1989. The published nonfiction discourse is limited during this phase. One piece, titled "Cloning," expressed concern that cloning techniques would bypass evolutionary mechanisms, which is a point expressed in Lederberg's original article. R. Trent, the article's author, said that when discussing the positive aspects of cloning a desired individual to enhance and preserve wanted traits, one should not forget that undesired traits are preserved as well. Thus, by limiting the genetic potential, one may increase those traits considered positive, but also many traits that might be considered negative. With strict cloning, and no genetic manipulation, you cannot take the good without the bad. Therefore, Trent finds that human cloning should not be done. "There are no rational arguments for cloning in the human. Cloning of cells is and will remain an important research tool. It should be taken no further than this in the human."[60]

Phase IV: Human Twinning Announced

At the end of this quiet period in the cloning debate, there was an explosion in writing on the topic. Actually, it is the effort of a bioethicist, Art Caplan, who brought the George Washington University twinning research to the attention of the press. Caplan called *The New York Times* when the twinning research was first announced. Before his call, the press either had not heard about it, or had chosen not to pursue the story. This demonstrates how much the field of bioethics had grown from the last phase, and also shows the change in where the debate took place. In the first three phases, most discussion took place through books, both fiction and nonfiction. Starting in the third phase, journals became the main platform for debate. The fourth phase introduces the media and cyberspace into the discussion. Communication of ideas and thoughts becomes almost instantaneous, and without peer review. This trend becomes most prominent in the fifth phase.

When Lederberg wrote his article, back in 1966, he warned against pursuing science without proper social reflection. He thought the pace of science would allow cloning to happen within a few years, not a few decades.

> Scientists are by no means the best qualified architects of social policy, but there are two functions no one can do for them: the apprehension and interpretation of technical challenges to expose them for political action, and forethought for the balance of scientific effort that may be needed to manage such challenges.[61]

> The implementation will doubtless proceed even without an adequate basis of understanding human values, not to mention vast gaps in human genetics.[62]

The latter statement reflects those parts of Lederberg's article that were frighteningly prophetic. Technologies such as in vitro fertilization and animal cloning show that those gaps did not need to be closed. Such procedures are more technology than science, meaning that one can make a baby or a clone without having the knowledge of what is going on. What has occurred is that reproductive technologies have become product-oriented, rather than knowledge-oriented. That may explain why many of the voices are from IVF circles, and not from basic scientists.

The early 1990s also saw a renewed interest in cloning fiction when almost all works were films. Audiences were treated to *Jurassic Park*, a movie in which dinosaurs were cloned from DNA remains. *Multiplicity* saw Michael Keaton clone himself. The clones were supposed to help around the house and take over his duties at the office, so he could have more time for himself. An episode of *Star Trek: The Next Generation*, "Up the Long Ladder," dealt with the idea of being cloned against one's will.

Besides an increase in the sheer number of voices in this round of the cloning debate, much of the literature took more of a legal stance than had been seen previously. The conversion from a theological and philosophical argument to a secular and legal concern is almost complete. Whereas only Carmen spoke on legal issues in prior phases, this era seems rife with concerns about legislating cloning and protecting procreative liberty. Perhaps much of this is the result of the fact that cloning had occurred in humans during this phase, which had not happened in earlier times (Rorvik being a possible exception).

The blind acceptance of da Vinci's machine metaphor of the body is an assumed model for biomedicine as well. Embryo manipulation to produce twins has occurred in humans, not just animals. Hoberman's article on the "technological image" of man was first presented at the University of Texas in Austin in 1986, several years before human twinning. In the titles of books, for example, *The Human Body Shop*, and the positions taken by thinkers, the assumption of the body as machine was evident. There was also a strong reference to writings of the past, for example, *Ethics for A Brave New World*, thus reinforcing that these discussions are ongoing and not unique. This also represents a period of time in which IVF and assisted reproduction was an everyday experience, to the point that national corporations, such as IVF America, have become common symbols. The body is not just a machine: It is also a factory.

The concerns and questions have changed little. The voices may come from different directions, but many opinions and arguments are familiar. Jeremy Rifkin and his Foundation on Economic Trends asked the NIH to freeze funding to research centers working on human cloning.[63] "This is the dawn of the eugenics era," Rifkin said, expressing the same sentiments that he had back in 1977 and again in 1983.[64] His concern was to prevent the use of cloning. Rifkin is one of the few people to have spoken during most of the major phases of the debate.

Daniel Callahan was quoted in the *Los Angeles Times* as saying that twinning threatens the idea of human identity[65]—an idea that was being discussed almost 25 years earlier by Ramsey.

In *Ethics for A Brave New World*, John and Paul Feinberg expressed concern over how statutory inheritance would work with a clone. For example, if a woman gave birth to her father's clone, would the clone inherit as the son or as the father? The Feinbergs also wondered what would happen if a couple divorced.

Would a husband have to pay child support for his wife's clone? Another fear they expressed was that clones could be used as spare parts, thus treating people as objects and as means only.[66]

"Current U.S. patent law makes patenting human embryos perfectly legal," said Andrew Kimbrell in *The Human Body Shop*.[67] Thus one could patent a series of clones from a famous person and peddle them, although such an act begins to smell of baby selling. The title of the book is suggestive of the machine metaphor, and Kimbrell seems to have intended a link. He warns against turning the human body into a car, an analogy made evident by the meaning behind the term "body shop:" (1) a place to have a car fixed; (2) a place to fix the human body. But is embodying the image of a car the best value to apply to the human being?

The year following the twinning announcement, 1994, was very busy for the publication of cloning articles. A special issue of the *Kennedy Institute of Ethics Journal* was devoted exclusively to cloning and twinning concepts. Many of the arguments made in this journal need to be reevaluated in light of Dolly. Like much of the pre-phase V literature, many propositions were based on the idea that real human cloning, especially nuclear transplantation, would never be feasible. Dolly has made such thinking obsolete.

Allen Verhey reflected on the discussion between Fletcher and Ramsey in the early 1970s. Verhey said that even though the technology is different (in fact, the technology did not exist in the 1970s), the issues were similar.[68] By presenting this comparison, he showed that few of the issues had been settled, even as the need for discussion had become more pressing. In the 1970s, IVF technology was not available, let alone cloning.

Another difference is that, in the 1990s, concerns over the covenant of parenthood seem less pressing as the debate shifts from the theological toward the machine metaphor. Machines, after all, do not have parents. With regular IVF (no cloning), one can have five parents,[69] and although troubling, this consideration has not prevented IVF from becoming a major business venture. The idea of a clone having seven parents seems to have been ignored.

Perhaps Fletcher and Ramsey were being alarmists in their contributions. Consider though, that the debate has been settled not by discussion, but by acceptance of technological reality.

Cohen and Tomkin, in their *Kennedy Institute of Ethics Journal* piece, felt that twinning would be great for IVF procedures. The two scientists said that, since one cannot clone differentiated body cells, concerns over cloning were unfounded.[70]

In the same journal issue, Howard Jones, another infertility specialist, found no reason to prohibit cloning. He thought that cloning had IVF applications, but was too expensive to be used on a regular basis,[71] which was the same sentiment expressed by Yoxen 10 years earlier. "What is needed at all levels of society," Jones et al. said in *Fertility and Sterility*, "is more discussion hopefully leading to an understanding that the purpose of all such efforts is to improve the human condition."[72] The problem with this statement is discerning what it would mean to "improve the human condition": Removing genetic disease, or infertility barriers to having children? Positive eugenics, selectively choosing certain traits as being more desirable, and then cloning those individuals so they represent a greater proportion of the gene pool? Or negative eugenics, preventing the less desirable from reproducing? An even bigger question, though, is who would make a decision as to what improvements are needed and as to what traits are beneficial.

Similar thoughts are echoed by Frances Kamm in the *American Philosophical Association Newsletter on Philosophy and Medicine*. She has several concerns about cloning: [73] Cloning would force society to create an ideal standard for a person; there may be a decreased value in the original (i.e., donor-parents), because they could be physically replaced easily (this concern reflects Leon Kass's 1985 article on the value of a person); and a government or business could breed people for special purposes, such as being soldiers or tough workers. One could literally be born to do a specific task. Such an idea goes directly back to Huxley, who imagined people twinned for specific purposes—

to perform particular jobs. Kamm's objections echo Lederberg and Ramsey.

According to George Annas, the commercial market has dictated much of the research and ethics in cloning, recalling Rifkin's ideas and fears from 1983.[74] If government regulation does not control a product, then the free market will. Unfortunately, this is the tradeoff: If one force does not control the technology, then the other will. Annas said that one needs to look at what is of prime importance, which for him is the welfare of the child (i.e., the clone). Concern about potential harm to the clone could necessitate a curbing of the market and require government regulation to protect people. He calls for a regulatory commission on human experimentation.

John Robertson, as a legal scholar, looks at cloning legislation, rather than at the free market. In his analysis, Robertson differentiated between twinning and nuclear cloning. Of twinning, he said, "There is no major ethical barrier to proceeding with further research in embryo splitting as a treatment or adjunct to IVF."[75] Twinning, for Robertson, falls under procreative liberty, which government, according to him, must respect. After all, Robertson states, without cloning (i.e., twinning), the cloned individual would not have existed: To exist is better than not to, in this scenario.[76]

On nuclear cloning, though, he takes a different stance. Robertson finds possible harms to the donor-parent and to the clone here, though he is mostly concerned with the clone's well-being. Robertson's concerns revolve more around social and psychological problems, rather than technical harms. Among the possible harms are unrealized parental expectations when the parents expect a clone to be just like the donor-parent. Clones might find it difficult if they are constantly misidentified as the original, or as other clones. He asks how would the donor-parent feel at being taken as one of his or her clones.

For Robertson in 1994, nuclear cloning does not fall under the rubric of procreative liberty.

> Reproducing with a cloned embryo may deviate too far from prevailing conceptions of what is valuable about reproduction to count as a protected reproductive experience.... Cloning exerts such a pervasive influence over the new individual [the clone] that it violates a basic sense of what makes reproduction valuable.[77]

The argument that Robertson makes here is the same one Ramsey had made: There is a difference between reproduction and procreation. This is a rare indication in modern cloning literature of a questioning of the machine metaphor. However, Robertson does not explicitly link his argument to how society views the human body.

The same issue of the *Kennedy Journal* also printed a report from the private think tank, the National Advisory Board on Ethics in Reproduction (NABER), which made several recommendations as to what cloning uses should and should not be permitted. NABER would permit cloning by embryo splitting to improve one's chances in IVF. Twinning could be useful if a couple had few embryos and needed more to improve their chances of a successful pregnancy and birth. The procedure could also minimize the number of egg retrievals that a woman would have to go through.

The group decided that cloning should be prohibited for the following purposes: donating embryos to others, "to provide an adult with an identical twin to raise as his or her own child,"[78] replacing a child who dies with one that is a twin, for spare parts, or for sale to others. The report stated that NABER was not in agreement on recommendations for two other possible uses: employing a twin for genetic testing before implantation[79] or having identical twins separated by time.

In another *Kennedy Journal* article, Ruth Macklin considers the potential cloning creates for loss of individuality, harm to the child, and "creating embryos for the purpose of genetic diagnosis."[80] It is only in these latter phases of the literature that concern about harm to the child-clone gains a predominant voice. Harm seems to be used as a sufficient reason for curbing freedoms and liberties in procreation and research.

Although harm has been a major concern throughout the entire history of the debate, the nature of that harm has altered. The harm was originally to society, humanity's relationship to God, and the meaning of the family. These issues have not been settled, but the subject of harm, in more recent literature, is the clone him- or herself. This alteration reflects a more general societal turn toward the rights of the individual, rather than toward obligations to the society. But it might also signal a shrinking moral discourse, an increasingly uncomfortable discussion of parent-child relations, families, and other concepts not easily reducible to individual rights or mechanical parts.

Macklin classified the response of bioethicists to twinning into three broad categories: "(1) Serious ethical concern; (2) Nothing ethically problematic; and (3) Guarded statements."[81] It is interesting that Macklin says "serious ethical concern," rather than "should ban cloning," since some statements certainly do fall into that category. Perhaps a fourth section, "do not clone," is needed to get a feel for the full range of opinions that have been expressed.

One person who would fit into the fourth category is Richard McCormick. His theological perspective represents a small resurgence of that point of view or a slight swinging back of the pendulum. Another explanation is that McCormick rejects the machine metaphor view of a human: thus, his concerns are with the larger issues of the place of the individual in the world, rather than taking that as a given. He has said that embryos deserve special respect because of their potential for becoming human life. This is an argument for the sanctity of life and the wholeness of the individual. "Perhaps we will begin to ponder what human cloning would be capable of doing to us, to our cherished sense of the sanctity, wholeness, and individuality of human life."[82] One way to examine this issue is to ask the question: if everything was changed about how a new human life is formed—where genes come from and how an embryo is created—would that new being still be fully human? When the discourse mentions surrogates and egg donors instead of mothers, and sperm donors instead of fathers, humans are objectified, and in the process, made to be less than individuals, less than human. The technology itself forces one to think in this way, since nuclear cloning requires an engineering or machine view of the body.

On the legislative front, in December 1994, the NIH issued a report on human embryo research. The report stated that the use and with special safeguards, the creation of human embryos for research was ethically acceptable. However, the panel did advise against funding research into twinning that would result in in utero transfer of a human twinned embryo. The report also suggested not supporting research into nuclear cloning.[83] President Clinton accepted the report, but rejected the recommendation on creating embryos for research purposes.

In 1995, Bonnicksen wrote that she believed twinning would likely appear in fertility clinics to help create genetic parenthood. But that does not mean the procedure should be done without any restriction. "Limits can be placed on its [twinning's] use, if not by legislatures, then by gatekeeping practices acting with an attitude of moderation."[84] Bonnicksen calls for a discourse on voluntarily limiting the clinical choices that twinning creates. Notice that she does not suggest legislation as a real solution, but calls for voluntary restraint. This has been a common theme in cloning. Instead of passing laws or taking a stand for or against cloning, any talk of restrictions is placed in terms of voluntary measures. President Clinton's 1997 ban on federal funding for cloning research affected federally funded projects only. However, because of bans in the 1980s on federal funding of embryo research, most cloning and embryo work takes place in private institutions. Clinton asked these groups to observe a voluntary ban.

Bonnicksen offered some guidelines to follow. She said that twinning should be limited to two twins—one splitting of the embryo—and that both twins should have to be implanted at the same time, eliminating the possibility of having identical twins several years apart. "The onset of spaced twins is social choice, not medical necessity."[85]

Other voices, such as Rosamond Rhodes, would put even fewer restrictions on cloning. "Our society's commitment to liberty requires that we allow individuals to make choices according to their own light and absent actual substantial evidence that such practices cause serious harm, we are not justified in denying individuals the option."[86] This argument is based on procreative liberty, and as Robertson pointed out, nuclear cloning may not fall under such protection.

Phase V: Sheep Cloning Announced

Phase IV ends with the February 24 *New York Times* article revealing Dolly's existence to the world. Although Dolly is a sheep, and not a human, her birth shows that the tools necessary for human cloning may be available, and that it may be only a matter of time until such a feat is attempted. The first wave of responses was on the whole condemnatory toward the idea of human cloning.

It is worth noting that the discussion of cloning, in the several months after the announcement, took place mostly on list servers, through news programs, and in news publications. Responses were swift, and the sound-bite became the medium through which ethical opinions were offered. The publication of journals and books would not come until later, since these modes of communication have longer time lags. With short-term turnaround through the popular media and on the internet, peer review and long, thoughtful consideration of topics are circumvented. Debates, even among scholars, take place in public. The lack of consensus on ethical and moral direction rapidly becomes evident.

Issues of biotechnology and ethics are no longer relegated to the halls of academia, but are the subject of popular discussions. The idea of the body as machine, whether in accepting cosmetically sculpted models as the idea of perfect beauty, or in watching athletes using technology to reach new records, has become an accepted norm. Thus, much of the literature that one sees is a general acceptance not only of cloning and genetic engineering in general, but of objectifying the human body and viewing it as a commodified machine.

In the press, though, after two months of heated debate and continuous discussion, the concern over cloning took a backseat. Or, one could say, once it was not front-page news, there was an apathy about cloning. The slow movement of cloning from page one to page four, and then to page 10 shows how quickly cloning had retreated to the back of the national mind. An April 1997 *New York Times* editorial is an example of this out-of-sight, out-of-mind phenomena. Titled, "Cloning as an Anticlimax: The Real Advance Came Decades Ago," the author says, "Cloning does not allow scientists to create anything new, it simply lets them copy something that already exists."[87] The thrust of the piece is that cloning is not so bad, because it does not genetically engineer anything new.

Yet, less than a year later the front page of the *New York Times* stated, "On Cloning Humans, 'Never' Turns Swiftly Into 'Why Not'."[88] A few days later that same newspaper published "Ethical Fears Aside, Science Plunges On."[89] A flurry of articles appearing in December 1997 could have been an attempt to examine the major news of the prior year, or it could have been evidence of the sort of apathy that Rifkin warned against: Given enough time, most scientific advances are permitted, and even praised.

Not only has the media shown that the public may be warming up to cloning, but a 1998 *Washington Post* article explained that a Chicago-area physicist, Dr. Richard Seed, said he had assembled the resources and the clients to begin cloning humans. The only thing he required to begin cloning was an infusion of venture capital.[90] Seed stated that he wanted to clone a human before Congress declared such an action illegal. If a law was passed banning cloning, then he intended to take his enterprise to Tijuana, Mexico.

Following Seed's announcement, though not motivated by it, 19 member countries of the Council of Europe voted to ban human cloning.

> 1. Any intervention seeking to create a human being genetically identical to another human being, whether living or dead, is prohibited.
>
> 2. For the purpose of this article, the term human being "genetically identical" to another human being means a human being sharing with another the same nuclear gene set.[91]

Several bills were proposed in the U.S. Congress as well. California had already prohibited human cloning in that state.

Further evidence of how cloning has entered everyday thought can be shown in a resurgence of cloning fiction. Television shows have dealt with the issue in such programs as *Star Trek: Deep Space Nine*, *Island City*, *The Outer Limits*, and even a miniseries. Books, such as Ken Follett's *The Third Twin*, have discussed the hazards of clandestine cloning. Movies have jumped on the bandwagon with cloning as a key component to the reappearance of the character Ripley in the film, *Alien Resurrection*. Even a Dilbert cartoon brought up the subject, with Dilbert having to prove that he had not been cloned.[92] *Time* and *U.S. News and World Report* both had special issues on the topic of cloning. Other magazines that covered cloning in great detail were *British Medical Journal, The Christian Century, Cq Researcher, Current Science, Economist, Fortune, Free Inquiry, Human Life Review, JAMA, Lancet, Maclean's, National Catholic Reporter, Nature, Newsweek, Reason, Science,* and *The Sciences*. Although not devoting special issues, most magazines had some cloning coverage, from *Ms*. to *Business Week* to *The New Republic* to *Playboy*.

Once enough time had passed for articles to be submitted and reviewed, academic journals began publishing on the topic of cloning. For example, *The Hastings Center Report* published a special issue in November-December 1997, which contained responses to the National Bioethics Advisory Commissions Report, *Cloning Human Beings*. The various articles presented concerns about, as well as support for, the report.

Nonfiction books were the last media platform to have capitalized on the Dolly phenomenon, with the first books published toward the end of 1997, and at the beginning of 1998. The first round of debate had already taken place in newspapers, televisions, and on the internet. Gina Kolata of the *New York Times* published a volume titled *Clone: The Road to Dolly and the Path Ahead*. Ronald Cole-Turner edited a book on *Human Cloning: Religious Responses*. Lee M. Silver authored *Remaking Eden: Cloning and Beyond in a Brave New World*. Other works include Gary McCuen's editing of *Cloning, Science and Society: Debating the Issues*, *Cloning* (At Issue) edited by Paul Winters, and Gregory Pence's *Who's Afraid of Human Cloning*. Even New Age metaphysics has become involved with the debate in books as demonstrated by Curt von Dornheim's *Angel Tears: Cloning and Genetic Engineering*.

In terms of the location of the cloning debate in the fifth phase, one sees almost a regression. In other words, whereas the discourse over the other phases had moved from books to journals and continued into the media and the internet, in the latest phase, the reverse has occurred. First was the media and the internet, followed by journals, and last, books.

Cloning and the National Bioethics Advisory Commission

In July 1996, the White House announced the initial membership of the National Bioethics Advisory Commission, or NBAC. The actual statement came late on a Friday afternoon in the middle of summer, which is precisely the time for an announcement of an event for which the least amount of press coverage possible is desired. NBAC held its first meeting that October, organizing itself around the specific tasks assigned it in the executive order that had been issued. The commission and its chair, Dr. Harold Shapiro, president of Princeton University, divided their assigned tasks into two parts: those concerning research with human subjects, and those concerning genetics. The commission immediately set to work, but their labors were decisively interrupted with the announcement of Dolly's birth, which was followed shortly by a letter from the President of the United States. The letter concluded with a request that NBAC "undertake a thorough review of the legal and ethical issues associated with the use of this technology, and report back to me within ninety days with recommendations on possible federal actions to prevent its abuse."[93]

The commission quickly revamped the next meeting's agenda to accommodate its new responsibility. A prominent biologist, Dr. Shirley Tilghman, was asked to explain the science behind Dolly, its significance and likely future uses, and its relevance to human cloning. Approximately one-half of that meeting was devoted to the testimony of, and conversation with, seven leading religious thinkers, spanning four major religious traditions: Protestantism, Roman Catholicism, Judaism, and Islam. Following that, four bioethics scholars presented a range of views on cloning, some arguing that it was clearly wrong, others that it might, under certain circumstances, be acceptable.

In time, the commission members recognized that the objections to cloning could be divided—crudely, perhaps, but effectively—into two rough categories. First were concerns about the risk of harm to any child who might be created by nuclear transplantation from another adult, as well as harm to the woman who would bear that child. Dolly was, after all, the only success out of 277 attempts. Furthermore, preliminary information about other, related techniques indicated that many such animals were developing abnormally, and that gestation and labor might also be abnormal. A study released by Wilmut and colleagues late in 1997 reaffirms the significance of safety concerns. Of lambs created by a less radical method—using fetal rather than adult cells—46 percent died in the perinatal period, and not a single ewe went into spontaneous labor.[94]

Although some commentators, including George Annas, complained that the commission was citing safety rather than ethical concerns, this criticism was mistaken. Preventing harm is clearly an ethical concern. Indeed, much of the literature on the ethics of research with human subjects focuses on risk, what is permissible, and what is not. By taking a stand against exposing human subjects to potentially serious risks, in the absence of extensive research with animal models, the commission was able to tie its rationale to a robust, half-century-long concern with the ethics of human subject research.

Safety concerns are tied directly to scientific evidence: If scientists are able to perfect animal cloning so that it adds little or no additional risk to the normal hazards of gestation and birth, then the safety concerns would dissolve. But that would not be the end of the story. Many people had concerns far greater, and much deeper, than safety. The commission had to confront those concerns as well.

The largely negative public response to human cloning had little to do with unethical human experimentation. Part of it, no doubt, was based on simple misunderstanding of what cloning would do—the photocopying myth, for example. The multitude of science fiction scenarios in which cloning is invariably portrayed as a mistake—sometimes horrific and evil, sometimes merely comic—undoubtedly contributed their own energy to public aversion. Beyond factual errors and fantastic scenarios, though, other serious reservations appeared. Some themes in religious ethics would seem to support human cloning, for example, that God gave humankind dominion over nature and commanded us to seek out knowledge. But many other threads in moral theology appear to warn against it: that it may be a denial or an affront to human dignity; that we are inclined to exploit that which we make; that cloning children would be a form of making or manufacturing, rather than procreating; that human dignity would be affronted because the child would be made a kind of object. Religious thinkers also raised concerns about the displacement of procreation through sexual union, about the moral inferiority of "making" to "begetting", of "reproduction" to "procreation". They also suggested that cloning would disrupt the integrity of the family, kinship networks, and familial lineages.

Some commentators, such as Gilbert Meilaender, suggested that cloning might somehow interfere with the cloned child's individuality. One way in which this might happen is that the child might be regarded, or might regard him- or herself, as having a constricted future, one whose boundaries have already been shaped by the previous carrier of that particular genome. This idea presupposes a fairly strong form of genetic determinism, and can almost certainly be dismissed on that ground alone. But such a dismissal might not convince the child or his or her parents. And, since the damage to the developing person is more a function of what people believe than of biological fact, the child's world might be diminished in just the way this argument describes.

Other ethical qualms concern what cloning might do to the relationships between parents and children, and to the values that underlie family life. In its report, *Cloning Human Beings*, the commission describes some of the worries attendant on the excessive control over a child's life that cloning may embody: "The lack of acceptance this implies for children who fail to develop according to expectations, and the dominance it introduces into the parent–child relationship, is viewed by many as fundamentally at odds with the acceptance, unconditional love, and openness characteristic of good parenting."[95] There was concern as well about harm to important social values. Values central to good parent–child relationships, such as love, nurturing, loyalty, and steadfastness, would be threatened by a practice which gives "implicit approval to vanity, narcissism, and avarice."[96] Finally, there were objections to treating people, especially children, as objects. The report states: "To objectify a person is to act towards the person without regard for his or her own desires or well-being, as a thing to be valued according to externally imposed standards, and to control the person rather than to engage her or him in a mutually respectful relationship."[97] Commodification—treating persons as things to be bought and sold in the marketplace—is a form of objectification.

On the other side, the commission also considered arguments in favor of cloning, generally of two kinds. First were arguments based on individual liberty and autonomy, especially reproductive liberty. The second set of arguments stems from our commitment to freedom of inquiry, in science as well as in other realms. Finally, the commission looked at cases in which the motives and consequences of cloning appeared to be relatively benign, such as its use in aiding infertile couples to have a child.

The commission's handling of ethical considerations in its report on cloning has received a mixture of praise and criticism. The report provides a strong argument that research on human cloning today is morally unacceptable given our current state of knowledge about its likely risks. On the other, more complex, ethical issues, the commission's strategy was to attempt to describe the most important concerns, and the reasons for thinking that each was coherent, plausible, mistaken, implausible, and the like. For the most part, the report does not take a stand on which of these broader moral concerns are well- or poorly founded, cogent or irrelevant. There was ample evidence of substantial disagreement among the commission members themselves on a number of these ethical issues. But then, 90 days is hardly enough time to give such complex concerns a full airing, let alone to reach consensus on each of them. This recognition, that deeper concerns needed to be widely and thoroughly debated, formed one of the grounds for the commission's recommendations.

In the first of five recommendations, the commission announced its conclusion that "at this time it is morally unacceptable for anyone in the public or private sector, whether in a research or clinical setting, to attempt to create a child using somatic cell nuclear transfer cloning." The recommendation gives two reasons. First, that such actions "would violate important ethical obligations were clinicians or researchers to attempt to create a child using these particular technologies, which are likely to involve unacceptable risks to the fetus and/or potential child." Second, "many other serious ethical concerns have been identified, which require much more widespread and careful public deliberation before this technology may be used."[98] The commission's other recommendations suggested an immediate voluntary moratorium for both federally and privately funded research into human cloning, federal legislation to ban such cloning—carefully constructed lest it unintentionally ban important (and morally unobjectionable) research with human DNA and cell lines—along with vigorous debate and public education. The commission also advised that any policies concerning cloning be revisited in three to five years to assess changes in social thought and technology in the near future.

Conclusion

In the nonfiction arena of the cloning literature, Lederberg set the style, pace, and points of argument that would be debated over the next 30 years. In each phase, authors came back again and again to the original points he discussed. One way of examining the literature is to see it as a series of variations and discussions on the issues outlined by Lederberg.

The most important element of the cloning discussion appears to be what are the risks and harms to the child-clone from the renucleation procedure. In the early 1980s, the debate shifted from talk about harm to social and religious institutions, such as the family and humanity's relationship to God, to talking about harm to the child-clone. The emphasis moves from the many to the one. From studies with cows, researchers know that calves created from fetal nuclear cloning have some metabolic problems. Although 60–70% of cow-clones are normal, 20–30% are up to twice as large at birth and need to be delivered by Cesarean section. However, within a few months, these large cattle do become normalized in terms of size. Ten percent of cow-clones have other problems, including joint disorders.[99] When added to the risk of harm to the clone of being built from old, and possibly mutated genes that could lead to genetic disease and malformation, the safety of cloning is in real doubt. Recall that Dolly was the only success in over 277 attempts to clone a sheep. Such numbers would be unacceptable in a human reproductive enterprise. If these risks cannot be drastically lessened, if not eliminated, then the dangers would satisfy the criteria put forth by Singer and Wells, Annas, Rhodes, and Robertson as conditions under which cloning could be restricted.

This is a story not of science, but of technology. The difference, in the modern age, is a fine one. Technology is the ability to construct objects and to create products. Science is the knowledge of how nature works. Without fully understanding embryo development, fertilization, and the whole process of procreation, reproductive technologists are capable of producing test-tube babies, artificial twins, and possibly nuclear clones. The tools that are used work, how they work, and what the implications are for individuals and society are unknown. Thus, when discussing donors and surrogates, one sees the language of commerce of production rather than a search for knowledge and understanding.

Along with the move of cloning from fiction to fact, and as a result of the development of the field of bioethics, the forum for debate has changed. The first publications, both fiction and nonfiction, were books in which detailed explanations of ideas and technologies had to be made anew each time. As a common language and knowledge base was established, shorter pieces could be published, since the wheel did not need to be invented each time. The debate moved to journal articles. Most recently, though, the discussion has left the academy and poured into the public arena. The media and cyberspace have become the predominant modes for expression. The danger in this is that words and ideas are put forth in soundbites, without the time for careful reflection and review by oneself and by one's peers. Careful inspection and detailing of arguments only appear well after the event, simply by nature of the time lag that journals and books necessitate.

The changes in the literature can also be viewed as a greater acceptance of the machine metaphor in human life. The debate begins with discussions over the meaning of life, family, and humanity's relation to the divine. Then it moves to a more secular view: How does the clone fit into the existing social and legal systems? Lederberg even fell prey to this line of thought when he suggested using clones for spare organs, or to clone an army of perfect soldiers. Each phase sees less questioning over the place and meaning of being human, and more acceptance that humans are truly replaceable cogs in a wheel.

Even the language used in ethical discussions reflects this idea of humans as machines. "Reproduction", "surrogate", and "donor" are removed terms that lack the emotional power and meaning of" procreation", "mother", and "father". The very process of reproduction needs to be taken out of the human context and objectified into the machine model, to enable one to even speak of it.

From its beginnings as a discussion of theology in fiction and then nonfiction, the adoption of the metaphor has pushed the literature into a more secular, legal, economic, and mechanical direction. Rather than talk about the meaning of family, the debate is on how a clone will inherit. Instead of concerns over whether humans should be interfering in procreation, assisted reproduction is an accepted norm driven by technology and society's acceptance of it. The move from the theological and philosophical to the mechanical and economic has foreshortened the debate on cloning. Rather than asking if one should clone, the question becomes when and how one should clone. However, the NBAC report takes seriously the earlier questions raised by Lederberg and Ramsey. This indicates a movement away from blind acceptance of the machine model, and a questioning of society's views of the body of and humanity.

Notes and References

[1]Huxley, A. (1950) *Brave New World*, Harper and Brothers, New York, p. 5.

[2] The term "clone" does not appear anywhere in Huxley's text. What he describes is not nuclear cloning, but more accurately, twinning.

[3] Kolata, G. (1997) With cloning of a sheep, the ethical ground shifts. *New York Times*, February 24, p. A1.

[4] Weiss, R. and Schwartz, J. (1997) Oregon scientists created primates from embryos not adult cells. *Washington Post,* March 2, p. A04

[5] Kolata, G. (1997) 10 Cloned cows soon to be born, company reports, duplicating a lamb experiment. *New York Times*, August 8, p. A10.

[6a] Clynes, M. E. and Kline, N. S. (1995) Cyborgs and space. *The Cyborg Handbook.* ed. C. H. Gray. Routledge, New York, p. 31.

[6] Weiss, R. (1998) Scientist will try to clone humans. *Washington Post*, January 7, p. A03.

[7] Haraway, D. J. (1991) *Simians, Cyborgs, and Women: The Reinvention of Nature.* Routledge, New York, p. 208.

[8] Ibid. p. 211.

[9] Hoberman, J. M. (1995) Sport and the technological image of man, in *Philosophic Inquiry in Sport, 2nd ed.* Morgan, W. J. and Meier, K. V., eds., Human Kinetics, Champaign, IL, p. 203.

[10] Ibid., p. 206.

[10a] McMurrich, J. P. (1930) *Leonardo da Vinci The Anatomist.* Williams and Wilkins, Balitmore, MD, p. 89.

[10b] Cartes, R. B. (1983) *Descartes' Medical Philosophy.* The Johns Hopkins University Press, Baltimore, MD, p. 100.

[11] Cohen, J. and Tomkin, G. (1994) The science, fiction, and reality of embryo cloning. *Kennedy Inst. Ethics J.* **4,** 193–204.

[12] Carmen, I. (1985) *Cloning and the Constitution*. University of Wisconsin Press, Madison, WI, p. xiii.

[13] Halacy, D. S. (1974) *Genetic Revolution, Shaping Life for Tomorrow.* Harper and Row, New York.

[14] Bonnicksen, A. (1995) Ethical and policy issues in human embryo twinning. *Cambridge Q. Healthcare Ethics* **4,** pp. 268–284.

[15] Cohen, J. and Tomkin, G. *Kennedy Inst. Ethics J.*, 196.

[16] Jones, H. W. (1994) Reflections on the usefulness of embryo cloning. *Kennedy Inst. Ethics J.* **4,** pp. 205–208.

[17] Voelker, R. (1995) A clone by any other name is still an ethical concern. *JAMA* **271,** p. 332.

[18] Diploid refers to a nucleus that has a full complement of chromosomes. In the case of humans, that means 46 chromosomes. Haploid refers to a cell with half the full set—only 23 chromosomes in humans—often in reference to a gamete (egg or sperm). Triploid means an unusual number of chromosomes are present, 69, and the cell will not develop normally.

[19] Halacy, p. 161.

[20] Briggs, R. and King, T. J. (1952) Transplantation of living nuclei from blastula cells into enucleated frogs' eggs. *Proc. Natl. Acad. Sci. USA* 455–463.

[21] Gurdon, J. B. (1962) Adult frogs derived from the nuclei of somatic cells. *Dev. Biol.* **4,** 256–273. *Also see* Gurdon, J. B. (1962) "The developmental capacity of nuclei taken from intestinal epithelium cells of feeding tadpoles. *J. Embryol.* **10,** 622–640. This was not adult nucleation since a tadpole is not the differentiated, adult form of the animal.

[22] Shettles, L. B. (1979) Diploid nuclear replacement in mature human ova with cleavage. *Am. J. Obstet. Gynecol.* **133,** 222–225.

[23] Hoppe, P. and Illmensee, K. (1981) *Science* **211,** 375.

[24] Baker, R. D. and Shea, B. F. (1985) Commercial splitting of bovine embryos. *Theriogenology* **23,** 2–12.

[25] Willadsen, S. M. (1986) Nuclear transplantation in sheep embryos. *Nature* **320,** 63–65.

[26] Prather, R. S., Barnes, F. L., Sims, M. M., et al. (1987) Nuclear transplantation in the bovine embryo. *Biol. Reproduction* **37,** 859–866.

[27] Stice, S. L. and Rob, J. M. (1988) Nuclear reprogramming in nuclear transplant rabbit embryos. *Biol. Reproduction* **39,** 657–664.

[28] Lewis, C. S. (1947) *The Abolition of Man.* MacMillan, New York.

[29] Lederberg, J. S. (1960) *The American Naturalist.* vol. 100, no. 915, Sept.–Oct. 1966, 519–531. Also appears in Lederberg, J. S. (1966) Experimental genetics and human evolution. *Bull. Atomic Scientists* **23,** 4–11.

[30] Ibid., p. 531.

[31] Ibid., p. 527.

[32] Ibid., p. 528.

[33] An idea that Ramsey acknowledged he got from Lederberg.

[34] Ramsey, P. (1970) *Fabricated Man.* Yale University Press, New Haven, CT, p. 88.

[35] Ibid., p. 87.

[36] Ibid., p. 89.

[37] The closest non-laboratory example of an event resembling cloning in nature is found in the concept of parthenogenesis. Although this has never been scientifically documented in humans, some stories of it do persist. For example, a woman in Germany, in 1944, caught in an Allied bomb attack, collapsed on the sidewalk. Nine months later she gave birth to a daughter who appeared identical to the mother, down to fingerprints and blood type. The examining physicians believed that the shock of the bombing may have triggered parthenogenesis in one of the woman's uterine cells. (Halacy, D. S. p. 160)

[38] McKinnell, R.G. (1979) *Cloning: A Biologist Reports*, University of Minnesota Press, Minneapolis, p. 105.

[39] Toffler, A. (1970) *Future Shock.* Random House, New York.

[40] Rosenfeld, A. (1972) Judaism and gene design. *Tradition* **13,** 71–80.

[41] Gaylin, W. (1972) The Frankenstein myth becomes reality—we have the awful knowledge to make exact copies of human beings. *New York Times Magazine*, March 5, pp. 20–221, 41–43, 48–49.

[42] Fletcher, K. (1974) *The Ethics of Genetic Control*, Anchor Books, Garden City, NY.

[43] Eisenberg, L. (1976) The outcome as cause: Predestination and human cloning. *J. Med. Philosophy* **1,** 318–331.

[44] Howard, T. and Rifkin, J. (1977) *Who Should Play God?: The Artificial Creation of Life and What it Means for the Future of the Human Race*, Delacorte Press, New York.

[45] Packard, V. (1977) *The People Shapers*, Little Brown, Boston, p. 141.

[46] Rorvik, D. (1978) *In His Image: The Cloning of a Man.* J. B. Lippincott, Philadelphia.

[47] Isaacs, L. (1978) The once and future clone. *Hastings Center Report,* (June 1978), 44–46, and Singer, P. and Wells, D. (1985) *Making Babies: The New Science and Ethics of Conception*, Scribners, New York, pp. 135, 136.

[48] Singer, P. and Wells, D. *Making Babies*.

[49] Subcommittee on Health and the Environment, Committee on Interstate and Foreign Commerce, U.S. House of Representatives. (1978) Developments in cell biology and genetics. (May 31), Government Printing Office, Washington DC.

[50] McCormick, R. A. (1978) Reproductive technology: ethical issues, in *Encyclopedia of Bioethics,* vol. 4, Reich, W. T., ed., Free Press, New York, p. 1462.

[51] Rosner, F. (1979) Recombinant DNA, cloning, and genetic engineering in Judaism. *NY State J. Med.* **79,** 1442.

[52] President's Commission for the Study of Ethical Problems in Medicine and Biomedicine and Behavioral Research (1982) *Splicing Life: The Social and Ethical Issues of Genetic Engineering with Human Research*, U.S. Government Printing Office, Washington DC.

[53] Yoxen, E. (1983) *The Gene Business, Who Should Control Biotechnology*, Harper and Row, New York.

[54] Rifkin, J. (1983) *Algeny*, Penguin Books, Harrisonberg, VA.

[55] Singer, P. and Wells, D., *Making Babies*, p. 149.

[56] Ibid., p. 149.

[57] Kass, L. R. (1985) *Toward A More Natural Science*, Free Press, New York.

[58] in Hyde, M. O. and Hyde, L. W. (1984) *Cloning and the New Genetics,* Enslow, Hillside, NJ.

[58a] Carmen, I., p. 35.

[59] Carmen, I. *Cloning and the Constitution*, pp. 191, 192.

[60] Trent, R. J. (1991) Cloning. *Bailliere's Clin. Obstet. Gynaecol.* **5,** 672.

[61] Lederberg, J. S., *The American Naturalist*, p. 529.

[62] Ibid., p. 530.

[63] Macilwain, C. (1993) Cloning of human embryos draws from critics. *Nature* **365,** 778.

[64] Elmer-Dewitt, P. (1993) Cloning: where do we draw the line. *Time* November 8, 69s.

[65] Callahan, D. (1993) Perspective on cloning. *Los Angeles Times,* November 12, p. B7.

[66] Feinberg, J. and Feinberg, P. D. (1993) *Ethics for A Brave New World*, Crossway Books, Wheaton, IL.

[67] Kimbrell, A. (1993) *The Human Body Shop*. Harper Collins, New York. p. 223.

[68] Verhey, A. (1994) Cloning: revisiting an old debate. *Kennedy Inst. Ethics J.* **4,** 227–234.

[69] Five parents: (1) the sperm donor, (2) the egg donor, (3) the surrogate, (4) the adoptive or raising father, and (5) the adoptive or raising mother.

[70] Cohen, J. and Tomkin, G., p. 193, 201.

[71] Jones, H. W. (1994) On attempts at cloning in the human, vol. 61, no. 3, pp. 205, 206.

[72] Jones, H. W., Edwards, R. G., and Seidel, G. E. *Fertility and Sterility*, p. 426.

[73] Kamm, F. (1994) Moral problems in cloning embryos. *Am. Philos. Assoc. Newsletter Philosophy Med.* **94,** 91.

[74] Annas, G. J. (1994) Regulatory models for human embryo cloning: the free market, professional guidelines, and government restrictions. *Kennedy Inst. Ethics J.* **4,** 235–250.

[75] Robertson, J. A. (1994) The question of human cloning. *Hastings Center Report* **18,** 12.

[76] Robertson, J. *Children of Choice*, Princeton University Press, Princeton, NJ, pp. 168, 169.

[77] Ibid., p. 169.

[78] National Advisory Board on Ethics in Reproduction (1994) Report on human cloning through embryo splitting: an amber light. *Kennedy Inst. Ethics J.* **4,** 271.

[79] Similar to the procedure where a single bud cell from an embryo is used for testing today.

[80] Macklin, R. *Kennedy Ins. Ethics J.* p. 221.

[81] Ibid., p. 215.

[82] McCormick, R. A. (1994) Blastomere separation. *Hastings Center Report* **14,** 16.

[83] NIH Advisory Committee (1994) *Report of the Human Embryo Research Panel*, September 27, NIH, Bethesda, MD.

[84] Bonnicksen, A. *Cambridge Q. Healthcare Ethics* p. 280.

[85] Ibid., p. 282.

[86] Rhodes, R. (1995) "Clones, harms, and rights. *Cambridge Q. Healthcare Ethics* **4,** 286.

[87] Boffey, P. M. (1997) Editorial: cloning as an anticlimax: the real advance came decades ago. *New York Times*, April 1, A22.

[88] Kolata, G. (1997) On cloning humans, "Never" Turns Swiftly Into "Why Not." *New York Times*, Dec. 2, A1, A24.

[89] Johnson, G. (1997) Ethical fears aside, science plunges on. *New York Times*, Dec. 7, wk 6.

[90] Weiss, R., Scientist plans to clone humans; anticipating ban, researcher says he has assembled doctors, volunteers. *Washington Post*, Jan. 7, 1998, p. A03.

[91] Council of Europe (January 12, 1998) *Additional Protocol to the Convention for the Protection of Human Rights and Dignity of the Human Being with regard to the Application of Biology and Medicine, on the Prohibition of Cloning Human Beings*. ETX. No. 168. Paris: 12.I.1998.

[92] Adams, S. (January 15, 1998) *Dilbert*. United Features Syndicate.

[93] Clinton, B. (February 24, 1997) Letter to Dr. Harold Shapiro, Chair, National Bioethics Advisory Commission.

[94] Schnieke, A., Kind, A. J., Ritchie, W. A., Mycock, K., Scott, A. R., Ritchie, M., Wilmut, I., Colman, A., and Campbell, K. H. S. (1997) Human Factor IX transgenic sheep produced by transfer of nuclei from transfected fetal fibroblasts. *Science* **278,** 2130–2133.

[95] National Bioethics Advisory Commission (1997) *Cloning Human Beings: Report and Recommendations of the National Bioethics Advisory Commission*, National Bioethics Advisory Commission, Rockville, MD, p. 67.

[96] Ibid., p. 68.

[97] Ibid., p. 71.

[98] Ibid., p. 106.

[99] Jones, H. W., Edwards, R. G., and Seidel, G. E., p. 424.

Abstract

The prospect of human cloning provides Congress with an opportunity to develop an effective regulatory mechanism for novel human experiments, and to begin to develop worldwide structures to oversee and regulate the new genetics. Human cloning should be banned, because replicating an existing human person would create the world's first human with a single genetic parent, and unacceptably threatens the resulting clone's personal identity and individuality. Cloning is replication, not reproduction, and is thus not protected by rights surrounding human reproduction and sexual activity. Only a ban can shift the burden of proof to scientists to demonstrate that there are vital reasons and safe ways to clone, before proceeding, and is the only effective way of giving society a voice regarding the application of technology that radically alters the very definition of what it is to be human.

The Prospect of Human Cloning

An Opportunity for National and International Cooperation in Bioethics

George J. Annas

I agree with President Bill Clinton that we must resist the temptation to replicate ourselves, and that the use of federal funds for the cloning of human beings should be prohibited. The prospect of human cloning provides an important opportunity to explore and define just what makes the prospect of human cloning so disturbing to most Americans, and what steps the federal government can take to prevent the duplication of human beings without preventing research involving the cloning of animals and human cells and tissues from proceeding.

The negative reaction to the prospect of human cloning by the scientific, industrial, and public sectors is correct, because the cloning of a human would cross a boundary that represents a difference in kind, rather than in degree, in human reproduction.

There are no good or sufficient reasons to clone a human, but that the prospect of human cloning provides an opportunity to establish a new regulatory framework for novel and extreme human experiments.

The Replication of a Human by Cloning Would Cross a Natural Boundary That Represents a Difference in Kind, Rather than in Degree, of Human Reproduction

There are those who worry about threats to biodiversity by cloning animals, and even about potential harm to the animals themselves. But virtually all of the reaction to the appearance of Dolly on the world stage has focused on the potential use of the new cloning technology to replicate a human being. What is so simultaneously fascinating and horrifying about cloning technology that produced this response? The answer is simple, if not always well articulated: Replication of a human by cloning would radically alter the very definition of a human being by producing the world's first human with a single genetic parent. Such replication threatens the loss of personal identity and individuality. Cloning a human is also viewed as uniquely disturbing, because it is the manufacture of a person made to order, because it undermines parental identity, and because it symbolizes science's unrestrained quest for mastery over nature for the sake of knowledge, power, and profits.

Human cloning has been on the public agenda before, and we should recognize the concerns that have been raised by both scientists and policymakers over the past 25 years. In 1972, for example, the House Subcommittee on Science, Research, and Development of the Committee on Science and Astronautics asked the Science Policy Research Division of the Library of Congress to do a study on the status of genetic engineering. Among other things, that report dealt specifically with cloning and parthenogenesis as it could be applied to humans. Although the report concluded that the cloning of human beings by nuclear substitution "is not now possible," it also concluded that cloning "might be considered an advanced type of genetic engineering," if combined with the introduction of highly desirable DNA to "achieve some ultimate objective of genetic engineering." The report called for assessment and detailed knowledge, forethought, and evaluation of the course of genetic developments, rather than "acceptance of the haphazard evolution of the techniques of genetic engineering [in the hope that] the issues will resolve themselves."[1]

Six years later, in 1978, the Subcommittee on Health and the Environment of the House Committee on Interstate and Foreign Commerce held hearings on human cloning, in response to the publication of David Rorvick's *The Cloning of a Man*. All of the scientists who testified assured the committee that the supposed account of the cloning of a human being was fictional, and that the techniques described in the book could not work. One scientist testified that he hoped that, by showing that the report was false, it would also become apparent that the issue of human cloning itself "is a false one, that the apprehensions people have about cloning of human beings are totally unfounded."[2] The major point the scientists wanted to make, however, was that they did not want any regulations that might affect their research. In the words of one, "There is no need for any form of regulatory legislation, and it could only in the long run have a harmful effect."[2]

Congressional discussion of human cloning was interrupted by the birth of Louise Brown, the world's first IVF baby, in 1978. The ability to conceive a child in a laboratory not only added a new way (in addition to artificial insemination) for humans to reproduce without sex, but also made it possible for the first time for a woman to gestate and give birth to a child to whom she had no genetic relationship. IVF is a striking technological approach to infertility; nonetheless, the child is still conceived by the union of an egg and sperm from two separate human beings of the opposite sex. Even though no change in the genetics and biology of embryo creation and growth is at stake in IVF, society continues to wrestle with fundamental issues involving this method of reproduction 20 years after its introduction. Since 1978, a child can have at least five parents: a genetic and rearing father, and a genetic, gestational, and rearing mother. We pride ourselves as having adapted to this brave new biological world, but in fact we have yet to develop reasonable and enforceable rules for even so elementary a question as who among these five possible parents the law should recognize as those with rights and obligations to the child. Many other problems, including informed consent, embryo storage and disposition, posthumous use of gametes, and information available to the child about the child's genetic parents also remain unresolved.

Viewing IVF as a precedent for human cloning misses the point. Over the past two decades many ethicists have been accused of crying wolf when new medical and scientific technologies have been introduced. This may have been the case in some instances, but not here. This change in kind in the fundamental way in which humans can reproduce represents such a challenge to human identity, and thus dignity, including the potential devaluation of the clone's life (even comparing the original to the copy in terms of which is to be more valued), that even the search for an analogy has come up emptyhanded.

Cloning is replication, not reproduction, and represents a difference in kind, not in degree, in the manner in which human beings reproduce.* Thus, although the constitutional right not to reproduce would seem to apply with equal force to a right not to replicate, to the extent that there is a constitutional right to reproduce (if one is able to), it seems unlikely that existing privacy or liberty doctrine would extend this right to replication by cloning.

* The usually insightful scientist R. C. Lewontin has challenged my testimony on this point, writing that, contrary to my assertion that the world's first clone would be "the world's first human with a single genetic parent." "A child by cloning has a full set of chromosomes *like*

There Are No Good or Sufficient Reasons to Clone a Human

When the President's Bioethics Commission reported on genetic engineering in 1982, in their report entitled *Splicing Life*, human cloning rated only a short paragraph in a footnote. The paragraph concluded: "The technology to clone a human does not— and may never—exist. Moreover, the critical nongenetic influences on development make it difficult to imagine producing a human clone who would act or appear 'identical.'[3] The NIH Human Embryo Research panel, which reported on human embryo research in September 1994, also devoted only a single footnote to this type of cloning. "Popular notions of cloning derive from science fiction books and films that have more to do with cultural

---

anyone else, half of which were derived from a mother and half from a father. It happens that these chromosomes were passed through another individual, the cloning donor, on the way to the child. That donor is certainly not the child's 'parent' in any biological sense, but simply an earlier offspring of the original parents." Lewontin, R. C. The confusion over cloning. *New York Review of Books*, Oct. 23, 1997, pp. 20,21 (emphasis added).

Lewontin makes my point about the difference between replication and reproduction in a different way. As he sees it, with cloning, you are your genes; and more than that, in terms of replication, you are nothing but a repository of your parents' genes. Thus, your parents can clone you the way they might split and embryo they had created with their egg and sperm. Children (even adult children) under this scenario have no say in whether they will be replicated, since they (the children) are not reproducing, their parents are. This would have to be true for future generations of clones as well, all of whom will have the same (dead) parents. Thus, children (including adult children) lose their right to decide whether or not to have children themselves (their parents retain this right) under this scenario. Moreover, after the clone's parents die, future clones would have to living parents at all. Whatever Lewontin's clones are, they are certainly not "like anyone else."

fantasies than actual scientific experiments." Both of these expert panels were wrong to disregard lessons from our literary heritage on this topic, thereby attempting to sever science from its cultural context.

Literary treatments of cloning help inform us that applying this technology to humans is too dangerous to human life and values. The reporter who described Dr. Ian Wilmut as "Dolly's laboratory father" could not have conjured up images of Mary Shelley's *Frankenstein* better if he had tried. Frankenstein was also his creature's father/god; the creature telling him: "I ought to be thy Adam." Like Dolly, the "spark of life" was infused into the creature by an electric current. Unlike Dolly, the creature was created as a fully grown adult (not a cloning possibility, but what many American fantasize and fear), and wanted more than creaturehood: he wanted a mate of his "own kind" with whom to live, and reproduce. Frankenstein reluctantly agreed to manufacture such a mate if the creature agreed to leave humankind alone, but in the end, viciously destroyed the female creature-mate, concluding that he had no right to inflict the children of this pair, "a race of devils," upon "everlasting generations." Frankenstein ultimately recognized his responsibilities to humanity, and Shelley's great novel explores virtually all the noncommercial elements of today's cloning debate.

The naming of the world's first cloned mammal also has great significance. The sole survivor of 277 cloned embryos (or "fused couplets"), the clone could have been named after its sequence number in this group (e.g., C-137), but this would have only emphasized its character as a produced product. In stark contrast, the name Dolly (provided for the public, and not used in the scientific report in *Nature*)[4] suggests an individual, a human, or at least a pet. Even at the manufactured level, a "doll" is something that produces great joy in our children, and is itself harmless. Victor Frankenstein, of course, never named his creature, thereby repudiating any parental responsibility. The creature himself evolved into a monster when it was rejected not only by

Frankenstein, but by society as well. Naming the world's first mammal-clone Dolly is meant to distance her from the Frankenstein myth, both by making her appear as something she is not, and by assuming parental obligations toward her.

Unlike Shelley's future, Aldous Huxley's *Brave New World* future, in which all humans are created by cloning through embryo splitting and conditioned to join one of five worker groups, was always unlikely. There are much more efficient ways of creating killers or terrorists (or even workers) than through cloning: Physical and psychological conditioning can turn teenagers into terrorists in a matter of months, rather than waiting some 18–20 years for the clones to grow up and be trained. Cloning has no real military or paramilitary uses. Even Hitler's clone would himself likely be quite a different person, because he would grow up in a radically altered world environment.

It has been suggested, however, that there might be good reasons to clone a human. Perhaps most compelling is cloning a dying child, if this is what the grieving parents want. But this should not be permitted. Not only does this encourage the parents to produce one child in the image of another, it also encourages all of us to view children as interchangeable commodities, because cloning is so different from human reproduction. When a child is cloned, it is not the parents who are being replicated (or are reproducing), but the child. No one should have such dominion over a child (even a dead or dying child) as to be permitted to use its genes to create the child's child. Humans have a basic right not to reproduce, and human reproduction (even replication) is not like reproducing farm animals, or even pets. Ethical human reproduction properly requires the voluntary participation of the genetic parents. Such voluntary participation is not possible for a young child. Related human rights and dignity would also prohibit using cloned children as organ sources for their father/mother original. Nor is there any right to be cloned that an adult might possess that is triggered by marriage to someone with whom the adult cannot reproduce.

Any attempt to clone a human being should also be prohibited by basic ethical principles that prohibit putting human subjects at significant risk without their informed consent. Dolly's birth was a 1-in-277-embryo chance. The birth of a human from cloning might be technologically possible, but we could only discover this by unethically subjecting the planned child to the risk of serious genetic or physical injury, and subjecting a planned child to this type of risk could literally never be justified. Because we will likely never be able to protect the human subject of cloning research from serious harm, the basic ethical rules of human experimentation prohibit us from ever using it on humans.*

Developing a Regulatory Framework for Human Cloning

What should we do to prevent Dolly technology from being used to manufacture duplicate humans? We have three basic models for scientific/medical policymaking in the United States: the market, professional standards, and legislation. We tend to worship the first, distrust the second, and disdain the third. Nonetheless, the prospect of human cloning requires more deliberation about social and moral issues than either the market or science can provide. The market has no morality, and if we believe that important values, including issues of human rights and human dignity, are at stake, we cannot leave cloning decisions to the market. The U.S. Biotechnology Technology Industry Organization has taken the commendable position that human cloning should be prohibited by law. Science often pretends to be value-free, but in fact follows its own imperatives, and, either

* This was ultimately the argument relied on by NBAC for its proposed five-year moratorium on human cloning by federal statue. National Bioethics Advisory Commission (1997) *Cloning Human Beings: Report and Recommendations*, Rockville, MD.

out of ignorance or self-interest, assumes that others are making the policy decisions about whether, or how, to apply the fruits of their labors. We disdain government involvement in reproductive medicine. But cloning is different in kind, and only government has the authority to restrain science and technology until its social and moral implications are adequately examined.

We have a number of options. The first is for Congress to simply ban human cloning. Cloning for replication can (and should) be confined to nonhuman life. We need not, however, prohibit all possible research at the cellular level. For example, to the extent that scientists can make a compelling case for use of cloning technology on the cellular level, for research on processes such as cell differentiation and senescence, and so long as any and all attempts to implant a resulting embryo into a human or other animal, or to continue cell division beyond a 14-day period, are prohibited, use of human cells for research could be permitted. Anyone proposing such research, however, should have the burden of proving that the research is vital, cannot be conducted any other way, and is unlikely to produce harm to society.

The prospect of human cloning also provides Congress with the opportunity to go beyond ad hoc bans on procedures and funding, and the periodic appointment of blue ribbon committees, and to establish a human experimentation agency, with both rule-making and adjudicatory authority in the area of human experimentation. Such an agency could both promulgate rules governing human research and review and approve or disapprove research proposals in areas such as human cloning, in which local institutional review boards (IRBs) are simply incapable of providing meaningful reviews.[5] The president's bioethics panel is important and useful as a forum for discussion and possible policy development, but we have had such panels before, and it is time to move beyond discussion to meaningful regulation in areas like cloning, in which there is already a societal consensus.

One of the most important procedural steps a federal human experimentation agency should take is to put the burden of proof on those who propose to do extreme and novel experiments, such as cloning, that cross recognized boundaries and call deeply held societal values into question. Thus, following the precautionary principle, cloning proponents should have to prove that there is a compelling reason to approve research on it and that this outweighs the likely harms. Congress can, and should, change the burden of proof for replicating humans by banning this use of cloning technology. I think the Canadian Royal Commission on New Reproductive Technologies quite properly concluded that both cloning and embryo splitting have "no foreseeable ethically acceptable application to the human situation," and therefore should not be done.[6] We need an effective mechanism to ensure that it is not.

Science, of course, is global, and we should also take this opportunity to work with other countries toward an international ban on human cloning, not just for its own sake, but as a practical precedent toward future international cooperation and regulation in the bioethics arena, especially in the area of human genetics and its applications. I agree with Dr. Ian Wilmut, that there are no good reasons to clone humans, and that we should work internationally to try to make sure it is not done. Thus, Dr. Harold Varmus's great fear of legislation and regulation is my great hope. The prospect of human cloning should provide an opportunity and precedent for the public, both in the United States and globally, to begin to take part in influencing the way science and medical technology shape our lives, our values, and our future as a species.

Acknowledgment

Adapted from Testimony on Scientific Discoveries and Cloning: Challenges for Public Policy before the Subcommittee on Public Health and Safety Committee on Labor and Human Resources, United States Senate, March 12, 1997.

References

[1] *Genetic Engineering: Evolution of a Technical Issue*, Nov., 1972.

[2] *Dev. Cell Biol. Genet.* May 31, 1978.

[3] President's Commission for the Study of Ethical Problems in Biomedical and Behavioral Research (1982) *Splicing Life: The Social and Ethical Issues of Genetic Engineering with Human Beings*, GPO, Washington, DC, 1982, p. 9, n. 5.

[4] Wilmut, I., Schnieke, A. E., McWhir, J., Kind, A. J., and Campbell, K. H. S. (1997) Viable offspring derived from fetal and adult mammalian cells. *Nature* **385,** 810–812.

[5] Annas, G. J. (1994) Regulatory models for human embryo cloning: the free market, professional guidelines, and government restrictions. *Kennedy Inst. Ethics J.* **4,** 235–249.

[6] Royal Commission on New Reproductive Technologies (1993) *Proceed with Care*, Canadian Communications Group, Ottawa, p. 741.

Abstract

This essay is concerned with two questions. First, is the cloning of humans beings morally acceptable, or not? Second, if it is acceptable, are there any significant benefits that might result from it?

I begin by drawing a distinction between two very different cases in which a human organism is cloned: The first aims at producing a mindless human organism that will serve as a living organ bank; the second, at producing a person. I then consider each of these in turn.

The moral issues raised by the former are the same as those raised by abortion. For this reason, I do not discuss such cloning at length, though I do indicate, very briefly, the reasons for thinking that it is not morally problematic.

The rest of the essay then focuses on the question of the moral status of cloning in cases in which the goal is to produce a human person. Here I begin by distinguishing between the question of whether such cloning is in principle morally acceptable, and the question of whether its use at the present time is morally defensible. The second of these questions I consider only briefly, but I do argue that the attempt to produce persons via cloning at the present time is open to serious moral objections. I then turn to the first question, and there I argue, first, that cloning that has the goal of producing persons is not intrinsically wrong; second, that such cloning would have a number of potential benefits; and, third, that none of the objections that have been directed against this sort of cloning can be sustained. My overall conclusion, accordingly, is that both sorts of cloning are in principle morally acceptable, and potentially beneficial to society.

The Moral Status of the Cloning of Humans

Michael Tooley

Introduction

Is the cloning of humans beings morally acceptable, or not? If it is acceptable, are there any significant benefits that might result from it? In this essay, I shall begin by distinguishing between two radically different cases in which a human being might be cloned, one in which the aim is to produce a mindless human organism that would serve as a living organ bank, and another in which the aim is to produce a person. I shall then go on to discuss the moral status of each.

My discussion of the first sort of case will be very brief, for the moral issues that arise in that case are precisely those that arise in connection with abortion. The second sort of case, on the other hand, raises very different issues, and it will be the main focus of my discussion. I shall argue that cloning of this second sort is in principle morally unobjectionable, and that, in addition, there are a number of ways in which such cloning would be beneficial.

Cloning: Persons, Human Beings, Organs, and Tissue

Cloning, in the broad sense, can be applied to very different things. One might, for example, clone a person's bone marrow, in order to use it in a transplant operation to treat a disease from which the person in question is suffering. Or one might, perhaps, clone some organ, though whether this is really possible in the case of structurally complex organs, such as the heart, is far from clear. In any case, such uses of cloning are both morally unproblematic, and obviously beneficial.

Most people would also think, I believe, that the cloning of nonhuman animals is not in itself problematic. Whether this is true for all animals is, however, not entirely clear. If, as some philosophers have argued, some nonhuman animals are persons, with a capacity, say, for thought and self-consciousness, then the moral status of cloning in the case of such animals would, presumably, be very closely related to the status of cloning in the case of humans.

Let us focus, however, upon humans. Here it is crucial to distinguish two different cases of cloning, since they give rise to very different moral issues. First, there is the case in which a human being is cloned to produce another human with the same genetic makeup as the original individual, and in which the human being thus produced is to serve as an organ bank, so that if the original individual loses an arm in an accident, or winds up with cancer of the liver, appropriate spare parts will be available. If the second human being were a person, it would, of course, be wrong to take parts from him or her to repair the damage to the original individual. The idea, however, is that something will be done to the brain of the human that is produced so that the human organism in question never acquires the capacity for consciousness, let alone the capacities that make something a person, such as the capacity for thought and self-consciousness.

Second, there is the case of cloning in which the goal is to produce a person, not a mindless organ bank. It is this latter type of cloning that is going to be the main focus of my discussion. Before turning to it, however, let me briefly touch on the former sort.

What objections might be directed against cloning that is done with the goal of producing an organ bank for some person?

One objection might be that if one were to use those organs, one would be using what belonged to someone else. Or, depending on what organs one was harvesting, one might even be bringing about the death of a human being. But here it is natural to reply that there is no person to whom the organs belong, or who is destroyed if the organism in question is killed. So no one's property is being taken from him or her, and no person is being killed.

How might one support this reply? The most familiar way of doing so is by appealing to cases in which a normal adult suffers brain damage that ensures that there will never again be any mental states at all associated with the human organism in question. Perhaps there is complete destruction of the upper brain, or perhaps all of the individual's brain has been destroyed, and the organism in question is now being maintained on a life support system. In such cases, would it be seriously wrong to terminate life processes in the organism in question? The vast majority of people seem to think that it would not be. But if that view is right, then it would seem that one needs to distinguish between something like the death of a person, the death of an individual who enjoys a certain sort of mental life, and the death of a human organism.

It is possible to maintain, of course, that the intuitions in question rest on an unsound view of human nature. Perhaps humans have immaterial, immortal souls that are the basis both of all their mental capacities, and of the states that make for personal identity. In that case, upper brain death, or even whole brain death, would not necessarily mean that there was no longer any person associated with the human body in question.

This is one possible view. But it is also a deeply implausible one, since there are facts about human beings, and other animals, that provide strong evidence for the hypothesis that the basis for all mental capacities lies in the brain. Thus, in the first place, there are extensive correlations between the behavioral capacities of different animals and the neural structures present in their brains. Second, the gradual maturation of the brain of a human being is accompanied by a corresponding increase in his or her intellectual capabilities. Third, damage to the brain, caused either by external trauma, or by stroke, results in impairment of one's cognitive capacities, and the nature of the impairment is correlated with the part of the brain that was damaged. These facts, and others, receive a very straightforward explanation, given the hypothesis that mental capacities have as their basis appropriate neural circuitry, whereas they would both be unexplained, and deeply puzzling, if mental capacities had their basis, not in the brain, but in some immaterial substance.

In addition, it is worth remarking, as a number of Catholic writers such as Karl Rahner and Joseph Donceel have pointed out,[1] that the hypothesis that an immaterial soul is added at the point of conception has, at least within Christianity, a very problematic implication, since most conceptions result, it seems, not in live births, but in miscarriages, and so the theological question arises as to the fate of those human beings who are never born. It seems unfair that they should wind up in hell. But equally, if they automatically went to heaven, that would seem unfair to humans who are born, and who, according to the New Testament, are more likely to wind up in Hell than in Heaven.[2] The traditional solution involves postulating a third after-life destiny—limbo—which, though originally rather unattractive, subsequently came to be conceived of as a place of perfect natural happiness. Even so, the idea that the majority of the human race never have a chance for eternal life in Heaven seems ethically rather troubling.

How do things stand if one sets aside, as implausible, the idea that an immaterial, immortal soul enters the body at conception? The answer is that, first, the distinction between a human organism and a person then becomes a very important one. But, secondly, that distinction does not in itself suffice to show that there is nothing problematic about cloning that is aimed at producing a mindless organ bank, since this still leaves the possibility of arguing that what is seriously wrong here is not the killing of a mindless human being, but the earlier act of permanently preventing the organism in question from developing a functioning brain.

What reasons might be offered for holding that the latter act is morally wrong? One possibility would be to appeal to an idea just considered, and rejected as implausible, namely, the idea that every human organism involves an immaterial immortal soul. For if that were so, then there would be someone whose interests might well be harmed, depending on exactly what happens to a soul in such a body, by the act of preventing the development of the brain of the organism in question. There is, however, a very different line of argument that one can offer, and one that does not involve the implausible assumption that humans involve immaterial souls, since one can claim instead that what is wrong about ensuring that a human organism can never develop a functioning brain is not that one is harming a person, but that one is thereby destroying a potentiality for personhood.

But is it morally wrong to destroy a potentiality for personhood? The following argument shows, I believe, that it is not. Compare the following two actions, the first of which involves two steps: One modifies an unfertilized human egg cell, or else a spermatozoon, or both, in such a way that, if the egg cell is fertilized by the spermatozoon, the result will be a member of our species that lacks an upper brain, and, thus, which will never enjoy any mental states whatsoever; one then brings about fertilization, and implants the resulting embryo. What about the second action? It involves taking a fertilized human egg cell, and changing it in such a way that it suffers from precisely the same defect as the fertilized egg cell that results from the first action. The argument now proceeds as follows. The person who holds that it is wrong to destroy a potentiality for personhood will certainly claim that the second action possesses a wrongmaking property—that of being an act of destroying a potentiality for personhood—which the first action does not possess. In response, it might be claimed that one is, in a sense, destroying a potentiality for personhood in the case of the first action as well as the second, and, thus, that, since the first action is not morally wrong, neither is the second. To this, however, one can reply that one needs to distinguish between active potentialities and merely passive potentialities: One has a passive potentiality for personhood when one has a situation that, if acted upon in appropriate ways, will give rise to a person; one has an active potentiality for personhood if one has a situation that will give rise to a person as long as it is not interfered with. The conclusion will then be that the first action involves the destruction of only a passive potentiality for personhood, but the second action involves the destruction of an active potentiality for personhood, and that it is only the latter that is wrong.

It may seem, then, that the defender of the view that it is wrong to destroy a potentiality for personhood has escaped the objection by reformulating the claim in terms of active potentiality. It turns out, however, that this response will not really do. In the first place, a fertilized human egg cell, on its own, does not involve an active potentiality for personhood: if left alone, it will simply die. If it is to develop into a person, it needs to be placed in an environment that will supply it with warmth, nutrients, and so on.

But, second, even if one waived this point, the above response still could not provide a satisfactory response to the above argument. The reason is that one can bring in a third sort of action, which is as follows. Suppose that artificial wombs have been perfected, and that there is a device that contains an unfertilized human egg cell, and a human spermatozoon, and in which the device is such that, if is not interfered with, it will bring about fertilization, and then transfer the fertilized human egg cell to an artificial womb, from which will emerge, in nine months' time, a healthy newborn human. Now one has a situation that involves not merely an almost active potentiality for personhood, as in the case of the fertilized human egg cell on its own, but, rather, a fully active potentiality for personhood. To turn off this device, then, and to allow the unfertilized egg cell to die, would involve the destruction of an active potentiality for personhood, and so that action would have to be wrong if the above, active potentiality principle were correct. But the action of turning off the device is not morally wrong, and so it follows that it is not wrong to destroy an active potentiality for personhood.

This argument could be countered if one had reasons for holding that human mental capacities, rather than being based on structures present in the brain, were dependent on the existence of an immaterial soul that God adds to a fertilized human egg cell, since, then, one could hold that it was really only after the addition of such an immaterial entity that an active potentiality for personhood was present. However, as we have seen, there is very strong evidence against the view that mental capacities have their basis, not in neural circuitry in the brain, but, instead, in some immaterial substance.

The terrain that we have just traversed, rather quickly, is very familiar, of course, from discussions of the moral status of abortion. Thus, discussions of abortion, or at least popular discussions, often begin with the claim that abortion is wrong, because it involves the killing of an innocent member of our species. The objection is then that there are cases in which an innocent member of our species is killed, but in which no injustice is done, namely, cases in which either the upper brain, or the brain as a whole, has already been destroyed. And so it is suggested that what is really wrong about killing, when it is wrong, is that a person is being destroyed. But if this is right, then one can argue that abortion is not wrong because the human that is killed by abortion has not developed to the point in which one has a person. This, then, typically leads, at least in the case of philosophically informed opponents of abortion, to the response that, while it is wrong to kill innocent persons, it is also wrong to destroy an active potentiality for personhood. And then, finally, one can reply, as above, that the potentiality principle in question cannot be correct, since it is exposed to counterexamples. For there are cases in which the destruction of an active potentiality for personhood is not morally wrong.

To conclude: The creation of mindless human organisms would be wrong if it harmed a person who inhabited, at some point, the human body in question, or if the destruction of an active potentiality for personhood were wrong. But there are good reasons for thinking that neither of these things is the case. In the absence of some other line of argument, then, one is justified in concluding that there is no sound moral argument against the use of cloning to produce mindless human organisms to serve as organ banks.

Cloning in the Present Context

Let us now turn to the question of the moral status of cloning when the objective is that of producing a person. I shall be arguing that cloning with that goal in mind is in principle morally acceptable. This, however, is not to say that such cloning would be morally unproblematic at the present time. And, indeed, I believe that there are good reasons why cloning, aimed at producing persons, should not be done at present.

To see why, let us begin by considering what was involved in the successful attempt by Ian Wilmut and his coworkers to clone a sheep from the cell of an adult animal:

> The investigators started their experiments with 434 sheep oocytes. Of those, 157 failed to fuse with the transplanted donor cells and had to be discarded. The 277 successfully fused cells were grown in culture, but only twenty-nine embryos lived long enough to be transferred to surrogate mothers. During gestation the investigators detected twenty-one fetuses with ultrasound scanning, but gradually all were lost except Dolly.[3]

Given these statistics, it seems clear that the idea of producing persons via cloning would not be a rational undertaking at present. What is irrational need not, of course, be morally problematic. But in the present case, one is considering an action that affects other people, and so one needs to ask whether it would be acceptable to encourage more than 200 women to be surrogate mothers in a situation in which it is likely that very few, if any, will have a successful pregnancy. And the situation is even worse if one is proposing cloning as a way of treating infertility: Given the present state of technology, the result will, in all probability, be enormous frustration and emotional suffering.

In response, it might be said that you pay your money, and you take your chances: If an infertile couple desperately wants a child that will be a clone of someone, how can it be immoral to allow them to try? But this argument could also be used in other cases, such as in that of providing those who are depressed, and who would like to commit suicide, with the means to do so. What I want to say, accordingly, is that if some course of action is very irrational, as, it seems to me, the attempt to have a child by cloning would be at present, then one may very well be acting immorally if one provides a person with the opportunity of performing that action.

But there are also other reasons for holding that the attempt to clone persons at the present time is morally objectionable—reasons that concern the individual who may result, if the attempt is successful. In the first place, the fact that only one of 277 pregnancies was successful in the case of the sheep suggests that something is seriously wrong with the procedure at present, and that, in turn, raises the question of whether there may not be a very significant chance, in the case of humans, that the outcome might be a seriously defective child, possibly born premature, but saved via intensive care. The attempt to clone a person, given the present state of the art, would seem to be wrong, therefore, because of the impaired quality of life that may be enjoyed by the resulting person.

Second, there is the unanswered question of how cloned individuals will fare when it comes to aging, because there is an important theory of aging that suggests that Dolly may very well have a significantly reduced life expectancy, as a result of having developed from the nucleus of a six-year-old sheep. Here is the basis of the worry:

> As early as the 1930s investigators took note of pieces of noncoding DNA—DNA that does not give rise to protein—at the ends of each chromosome, which they called telomeres (from the Greek words for "end" and "part"). When the differentiated cells of higher organisms undergo mitosis, the ordinary process of cell division, not all of the DNA in their nuclei is replicated. The enzyme that copies DNA misses a small piece at the ends of each chromosome, and so the chromosomes get slightly shorter each time a cell divides. As long as each telomere remains to buffer its chromosome against the shortening process, mitosis does not bite into any genes (remember that the telomeres are noncoding, much like the leaders at the ends of a reel of film). Eventually, however, the telomeres get so short that they can no longer protect the vital parts of the chromosome. At that point the cell usually stops dividing and dies.[4]

The question, accordingly, is whether Dolly started life with cells whose chromosomes have telomeres whose length is comparable to those in the cells of a six-year-old sheep. Perhaps not, since it may be that, once a nucleus has been transplanted into an egg from which the nucleus has been removed, there is some mechanism that will produce an enzyme, called telomerase, that can create full-length telomeres. But the risk is surely a very serious one, and this provides strong grounds, I suggest, for holding that one should not at this point attempt to produce people by cloning.

The last two reasons also support a stronger conclusion, namely, that there are grounds for a temporary, legal prohibition on the cloning of humans when the goal is to produce persons. The risk that is involved in such cloning is that one will bring into existence a person who will age prematurely, or who will suffer from other defects. What is at stake are potential violations of an individual's rights, and thus something that justifies the introduction of appropriate legislation.

The qualification here perhaps needs to be emphasized: This conclusion applies only to cloning that is directed at producing a person, since, if one's goal were instead to produce a mindless human organism to serve as an organ bank, the above considerations would not apply.

Is It Intrinsically Wrong to Produce a Person by Cloning?

Let us now turn to the question of whether the use of cloning to produce a person is, in principle, morally acceptable or not. In this section, I shall focus on the question of whether cloning, so used, is intrinsically wrong. Then, in a later section, I shall consider whether cloning to produce persons necessarily has consequences that render it morally wrong.

How might one attempt to argue that the production of persons via cloning is intrinsically wrong? Here it seems to me that Dan Brock is right when he suggests that there are basically two lines of argument that deserve examination.[5] First, there is an argument that appeals to what might initially be described as the right of a person to be a unique individual, but which, in the end, must be characterized instead as the right of a person to a genetically unique nature. Second, there is an argument that appeals to the idea that a person has a right to a future that is, in a certain sense, open.

Does a Person Have a Right to a Genetically Unique Nature?

Many people feel that being a unique individual is important, and the basic thrust of this first attempt to show that cloning is intrinsically wrong involves the idea that the uniqueness of individuals would be in some way impaired by cloning. In response, I think that one might very well question whether uniqueness is important. If, for example, it turned out that there was, perhaps on some distant planet, an individual that was qualitatively identical to oneself, down to the last detail, both physical and psychological, would that really make one's own life less valuable, less worth living?

In thinking about this issue, it may be important to distinguish two different cases: first, the case in which the two lives are qualitatively identical because of the operation of deterministic causal laws; second, the case in which it just happens that both individuals are always in similar situations in which they freely decide upon the same actions, have the same thoughts and feelings, and so on. The second of these scenarios, I suggest, is not troubling. The first, on the other hand, may be. But if it is, is it because there is a person who is qualitatively indistinguishable from oneself, or, rather, because one's life is totally determined?

I am inclined to question, accordingly, the perhaps rather widely held view that uniqueness is an important part of the value of one's life. Fortunately, however, one need not settle that issue in the present context, since cloning does not, of course, produce a person who is qualitatively indistinguishable from the individual who has been cloned, for, as is shown by the case of identical twins, two individuals with the same genetic makeup, even if raised within the same family at the same time, will differ in many respects, because of the different events that make up their life histories.

How great are those differences? The result of one study was as follows:

> On average, our questionnaires show that the personality traits of identical twins have a 50 percent correlation. The traits of fraternal twins, by contrast, have a correlation of 25 percent, non-twin siblings a correlation of 11 percent and strangers a correlation of close to zero.[6]

Consequently, the personality traits of an individual and his or her clone should, on average, exhibit no more than a 50 percent correlation, and, presumably, the correlation will generally be even less, given that an individual and his or her clone will typically be raised at different times, and in generations that may differ quite substantially in terms of basic beliefs and fundamental values.

The present argument, accordingly, if it is to have any chance, must shift from an appeal to the claim that a person has a right to absolute uniqueness to an appeal to the very different claim that a person has a right to a genetically unique nature. How, then, does the argument fare when reformulated in that way?

An initial point worth noticing is that any appeal to a claimed right to a genetically unique nature poses a difficulty for a theist: if there is such a right, why has God created a world where identical twins can arise? But there are, of course, many features of the world that are rather surprising, if our world is one that was created by an omnipotent, omniscient, and morally perfect person, and so the theist who appeals to a right to a genetically unique nature may simply reply that the presence of twins is just another facet of the general problem of evil.

How can one approach the question of whether persons have a right to a genetically unique nature? Some writers, I think, are content to rest with a burden of proof approach. Here the idea is that, although it may be the case that many people do think that being a unique individual, in the sense of not being qualitatively identical with anyone else, is an important part of what is valuable about being a person, the idea that persons have a right to a genetically unique identity is one that, by contrast, has been introduced only recently, and so those who advance the latter claim really need to offer some reason for thinking that it is true.

There are, however, other ways of approaching this question that involve offering positive arguments against the claim. One possibility, for example, is to appeal to the intuitions that one has upon reflection. Thus, one can consider the case of identical twins, and ask oneself whether, upon reflection, one thinks that it would be prima facie wrong to reproduce if one somehow knew that doing so would result in identical twins. I think it would be surprising if many people felt that this was so.

Another way of approaching the issue is by appealing to some plausible general theory of rights. Thus, for example, I am inclined to think that rights exist when there are serious, self-regarding interests that deserve to be protected. If some such view is correct, then one can approach the question of whether persons have a right to a genetically unique nature by asking whether one has some serious, self-regarding interest that would be impaired if one were a clone. Is the latter the case? The initial reason for thinking that it is not is that the existence of a clone does not seem to impinge on a person in the same way in which being prevented from performing some action that harms no one, or being tortured, or being killed, does: A distant clone might have no impact at all upon one's life.

In response, it might be argued that, while the mere existence of a clone need have no impact on, and so need not impair in any way, one's self-regarding interests, the situation might be very different if one knew of the existence of the clone, since that knowledge might, for example, be damaging to one's sense of individuality. But why should this be so, given that individuals can differ greatly, although sharing the same genetic makeup? It seems to me that if the knowledge that a clone of oneself exists were disturbing to one, this would probably be because of the presence of some relevant, false belief, such as a belief in genetic determinism. But if this is so, then the question arises as to whether rights exist when the interests that they protect are ones that will be harmed only if the potential subjects of the harm have certain false, and presumably irrational, beliefs. My own feeling is that the responsibility for such harm is properly assigned to the individual who has acquired the irrational beliefs whose presence is necessary if there is to be any harm. Consequently, it seems to me that the actions of others should not be constrained in order to prevent such harm from occurring, and thus that there is no right that is violated in such a case.

A third way of thinking about this question of whether there is a right to a genetically unique nature is to consider a scenario in which individuals with the same genetic makeup are very common indeed, and to consider whether such a world would, for example, be inferior to the present world. Imagine, for example, that it is the year 4004 BC, and that God is contemplating creating human beings. He has already considered the idea of letting humans come into being via evolution, but has rejected that plan on the grounds that a lottery approach to such a vital matter as bringing humans into existence hardly seems appropriate. He also considers creating an original human pair that are genetically distinct, and who will then give rise to humans who will be genetically quite diverse. Upon reflection, however, that idea also seems flawed, since the random shuffling of genes will result in individuals who may be physically impaired, or disposed to unpleasant diseases, such as cancer, that will cause them enormous suffering and lead to premature deaths. In the end, accordingly, the Creator decides upon a genetic constitution with the following two properties. First, it will not lead to serious physical handicaps and diseases, and it will allow an individual, who makes wise choices, to grow in mind and spirit. Second, all of the genes involve identical alleles. God then creates one person with that genetic makeup—call her Eve—and a second individual, Adam, whose only genetic difference is that he has one X chromosome, and one Y chromosome, where Eve has two X chromosomes. The upshot will then be that when Adam and Eve reproduce, they will breed true, because of the fact that they have, aside from the one difference, the same genetic makeup, with identical alleles for every inherited character, and so all of their descendants will be genetically identical to either Adam or Eve.

How would such a world compare with the actual world? If one were choosing from behind the Rawlsian veil of ignorance, would it be rational to prefer the actual world, or the alternative world? This is not, perhaps, an easy question. But it is clear that there would be some significant pluses associated with the alternative world. First, unlike the actual world, one would be assured of a genetic makeup that would be free of dispositions to various unwelcome and life-shortening diseases, or to other debilitating conditions such as depression, schizophrenia, and so on. Secondly, inherited traits would be distributed in a perfectly equitable fashion, and no one would start out, as is the case in the actual world, severely disadvantaged, and facing an enormous uphill battle. Third, aside from the differences between men and women, everyone would be physically the same, and so people would differ only with regard to the quality of their "souls", and thus one would have a world in which judgments of people might well have a less superficial basis than is often the case in the actual world. So there would seem to be some serious reasons for preferring the alternative world over the actual world.

The third advantage just mentioned also points, of course, to an obvious practical drawback of the alternative world: knowing who was who would be a rather more difficult matter than it is in the actual world. But this problem can be dealt with by variants on the above scenario. One variant, for example, would involve having identity of genetic makeup, except regarding the genes that determine the appearance of face and hair. Then one would be able to identify individuals in just the way that one typically does in the actual world. This change would mean, of course, that one was no longer considering an alternative world in which there was widespread identity with respect to genetic makeup. Nevertheless, if this other alternative world would be preferable to the actual world, I think that it still provides an argument against the view that individuals have a right to a unique genetic makeup. For, first of all, the preferability of this other alternative world strongly suggests that genetic difference, rather than being desirable in itself, is valuable only to the extent that it is needed to facilitate the easy identification of people. Second, is it plausible to hold that, although genetic uniqueness is crucial, a very high degree of genetic similarity is not? But in the alternative world we are considering here, the degree of genetic similarity between any two individuals would be extraordinarily high. Third, the alternative world is one in which the genes that determine the initial structure of one's brain are not merely very similar, but absolutely the same in all individuals. But, then, can one plausibly hold that genetic uniqueness is morally crucial, while conceding that a world in which individuals do not differ regarding the genes that determine the initial nature of their brains might be better than the actual world?

These three considerations, I suggest, provide good reasons for holding that one cannot plausibly maintain that individuals have a right to a genetically unique nature, without also holding that the actual world is to be preferred to the alternative world just described. The identification problem can, however, also be addressed without shifting to a world where people differ genetically, since one could instead suppose that a different mechanism for identifying other people is built into human beings. God could, for example, incorporate special circuitry into the human brain, which broadcasts both one's name and appropriate identifying information about one, and which picks up the information that is broadcast by other humans within one's perceptual field. The information is then checked against a memory bank containing information about everyone one knows, and if it turns out that one is in perceptual contact with some person with whom one is acquainted, and if one would like to know who the person in question is, one would automatically find oneself in possession of the relevant information.

The result would be a world where all individuals will have exactly the same genetic makeup, aside from an X and a Y chromosome, and all of the attractive features of the original alternative world would be present, without there being any problem of determining who was who. One can then ask how this world compares with the actual world, and whether, in particular, the fact that all people in this alternative world would have essentially the same genetic makeup really seems to be, upon reflection, a reason for preferring the actual world.

The Open Future Argument

Dan Brock mentions a second argument for the view that cloning that aims at producing persons is intrinsically wrong.[7] The argument, which is based upon ideas put forward by Joel Feinberg, who speaks of a right to an open future,[8] and by Hans Jonas, who refers to a right to ignorance of a certain sort[9], is essentially as follows. One's genetic makeup may very well determine to some extent the possibilities that lie open to one, and so it may constrain the course of one's future life. If there is no one with the same genetic makeup, or if there is such a person, but one is unaware of the fact, or, finally, if there is such a person, but the person is either one's contemporary, or someone who is younger, then one will not be able to observe the course of the life of someone with the same genetic makeup as oneself. But what if one does know of a genetically identical person whose life precedes one's own? Then one could have knowledge that one might well view as showing that certain possibilities were not really open to one, and so one would have less of a sense of being able to choose the course of one's life.

To see why this argument is unsound, one needs to ask about the reasoning that might be involved if someone, observing the earlier life of someone with the same genetic makeup, concludes that his or her own life is subject to certain constraints. One possibility is that one may have observed someone striving very hard, over a long period of time, to achieve some goal and failing to get anywhere near it. Perhaps the earlier, genetically identical individual wanted to be the first person to run the marathon in under two hours, and after several years of intense and well-designed training, attention to diet, and so on, never got below two and one-half hours. One would then surely be justified in viewing that particular goal as not really open to one. But would that knowledge be a bad thing, as Jonas seems to be suggesting? I would think that, on the contrary, such knowledge would be valuable, since it would make it easier for one to choose goals that one could successfully pursue.

A very different possibility is that one might observe the course of the life of the genetically identical individual, and conclude that no life significantly different from that life could really be open to one. Then one would certainly feel that one's life was constrained to a very unwelcome extent. But in drawing the conclusion that one's life could not be significantly different from that of the other individual, one would be drawing a conclusion for which there is not only no evidence, but one that there is excellent evidence against: The lives of identical twins demonstrate that very different lives indeed are possible, given the same genetic makeup.

In short, the idea that information about the life of a person genetically identical to oneself would provide grounds for concluding that only a narrow range of alternatives was open to one would only be justified if genetic determinism, or a close approximation thereto, was correct. But nothing like genetic determinism is true. This second argument for the view that cloning with the goal of producing persons is intrinsically wrong is, accordingly, unsound.

Considerations in Support of the Cloning of Persons

Whether it is desirable to produce persons by cloning depends, as we noticed earlier, upon the outcome of an issue that is not yet decided: the aging question. Here, however, I shall simply assume that it will become possible to clone an adult individual in such a way that one winds up with a cell whose chromosomes have full-length telomeres, so that the individual who results will have a normal life expectancy. Given that assumption, I want to argue that there are a number of important benefits that may result from the cloning of humans that is done with the goal of producing persons.

In setting out what I take to be benefits of cloning, I shall not address possible objections. These will be discussed, instead, under "Objections to the Cloning of Humans."

Scientific Knowledge: Psychology and the Heredity-vs-Environment Issue

A crucial theoretical task for psychology is the construction of a satisfactory theory that will explain the acquisition of traits of character, and central to the development of such a theory is information about the extent to which various traits are inherited, or alternatively, dependent on aspects of the environment that are controllable, or, finally, dependent on factors, either in the brain or in the environment, that have a chancy quality. But such knowledge is not just theoretically crucial to psychology. Knowledge of the contributions that are, and are not, made to the individual's development by his or her genetic makeup, by the environment in which he or she is raised, and by chance events, will enable one to develop approaches to childrearing that will increase the likelihood that one can raise people with desirable traits, people who will have a better chance of realizing their potentials, and of leading happy and satisfying lives. So this knowledge is not merely of great theoretical interest: it is also potentially very beneficial to society.

In the attempt to construct an adequate theory of human development, the study of identical twins has been very important, and has generated considerable information on the nature/nurture issue. But adequate theories still seem rather remote. Cloning would provide a powerful way of speeding up scientific progress in this area, since society could produce a number of individuals with the same genetic makeup, and then choose adoptive parents who would provide those individuals with good, but significantly different environments, in which to mature.

Cloning to Benefit Society

One very familiar suggestion is that one might benefit mankind by cloning individuals who have made very significant contributions to society. In the form in which it is usually put, when it is assumed that, if, for example, one had been able to clone Albert Einstein, the result would be an individual who would also make some very significant contribution to science, the suggestion is surely unsound. In the first place, whether an individual will do highly creative work surely depends on traits whose acquisition is a matter of the environment in which the individual is raised, rather than on being determined simply by his or her genetic makeup. But could it not be argued in response that one could control the environment as well, raising a clone of Einstein, for example, in an environment that was as close as possible to the sort of environment in which Einstein was raised? That, of course, might prove difficult. But even if it could be done, it is not clear that it would be sufficient, because there is a second point that can be made here, namely, that great creative achievements may depend on things that are to some extent accidental, and whose occurrence is not ensured by the combination of a certain genetic makeup and a certain general sort of environment. Many great mathematicians, for example, have developed an intense interest in numbers at an early age. Is there good reason to think that, had one been able to clone Carl Friedrich Gauss, and reared that person in an environment similar to Gauss's, that person would have developed a similar interest in numbers, and gone on to achieve great things in mathematics? Or is it likely that a clone of Einstein, raised in an environment similar to that in which Einstein was raised, would have wondered, as Einstein did, what the world would look like if one could travel as fast as light, and then gone on to reflect on the issues that fascinated Einstein, and that led ultimately to the development of revolutionary theories in physics?

I think that there are, then, some serious problems with the present suggestion in the form in which it is usually put. On the other hand, I am not convinced that a slightly more modest version cannot be sustained. Consider, for example, the Polgar sisters. There we have a case in which the father of three girls succeeded in creating an environment in which all three of his daughters became very strong chess players, and one of them, Judit Polgar, is now the strongest female chess player who has ever lived. Is it not reasonable to think that if one were to make a number of clones of Judit Polgar, and then raise them in an environment very similar to that in which the Polgar sisters were raised, the result would be a number of very strong chess players?

More generally, I think it is clear that there is a strong hereditary basis for intelligence,[10] and I also believe that there is good reason for thinking that other traits that may play a crucial role in creativity, such as extreme persistence, determination, and confidence in one's own abilities, are such as are likely to be produced by the right combination of heredity and environment. So, although the chance that the clone of an outstandingly creative individual will also achieve very great things is perhaps, at least in many areas, not especially high, I think that there is reason for thinking that, given an appropriate environment, the result will be an individual who is likely to accomplish things that may benefit society in significant ways.

Happier and Healthier Individuals

A third benefit of cloning is that it should make it possible to increase the likelihood that the person that one is bringing into existence will enjoy a healthy and happy life. For, to the extent that one's genetic constitution has a bearing on how long one is likely to live, on what diseases, both physical and mental, one is likely to suffer from, and on whether one will have traits of character or temperament that make for happiness, or for unhappiness, by cloning a person who has enjoyed a very long life, who has remained mentally alert, and not fallen prey to Alzheimer's disease, who has not suffered from cancer, arthritis, heart attacks, stroke, high blood pressure, and so on, and who has exhibited no tendencies to depression, or schizophrenia, and so on, one is increasing the chances that the individual that one is producing will also enjoy a healthy and happy life.

More Satisfying Childrearing: Individuals with Desired Traits

Many couples would prefer to raise children who possess certain traits. In some cases they may want children who have a certain physical appearance. In other cases, they might like to have children who have the physical abilities that would enable them to have a better chance of performing at a high level in certain physical activities. Or they might prefer to have children who would have the intellectual capabilities that would enable them to enjoy mathematics or science. Or they might prefer to have children who possess traits that would enable them to engage in, and enjoy, various aesthetic pursuits. Some of the traits that people might like their children to have presumably have a very strong hereditary basis; others are such as a child, given both the relevant genes, and the right environment, would be very likely to acquire. To the extent that the traits in question fall into either of these categories, the production of children via cloning would enable more couples to raise children with traits that they judge to be desirable.

More Satisfying Childrearing: Using Self-Knowledge

There is a second way in which cloning could make childrearing more satisfying, and it emerges if one looks back on one's own childhood. Most people, when they do this, remember things that they think were good, and other things that they think would have been better if they had been different. In some cases, of course, one's views may be unsound, and it may be that some of the things that one's parents did, and which one did not like, actually had good effects on one's development. On the whole, however, it seems plausible that most people have reasonably sound views on which features of the way in which they were raised had good effects overall, and which did not.

The idea, then, is that if a couple raises a child who is a clone of one of the parents, the knowledge that the relevant parent has of the way in which he or she was raised can be used to bring up the child in a way that fits better with the individual psychology of the child. In addition, given the greater psychological similarity that will exist between the child and one of his parents in such a case, the relevant parent will better be able, at any point, to appreciate how things look from the child's point of view. So it would seem that there is a good chance both that such a couple will find childrearing a more rewarding experience, and that the child will have a happier childhood through being better understood.

Infertility

Since the successful cloning that resulted in Dolly, at least one person has expressed the intention of pushing ahead with the idea of using cloning to help infertile couples. For reasons that emerged under the second heading, "Cloning in the Present Context", the idea that cloning should be so used in the near future seems morally very problematic. In principle, however, the general idea would seem to have considerable merit. One advantage, for example, as Dan Brock and others have pointed out, is that "cloning would allow women who have no ova or men who have no sperm to produce an offspring that is biologically related to them."[11] Another advantage, also noted by Brock, is that "embryos might be cloned, either by nuclear transfer or embryo splitting, in order to increase the number of embryos for implantation and improve the chances of successful conception."[12]

Children for Homosexual Couples

Many people, especially in the United States, believe that homosexuality is deeply wrong, and that homosexuals should not be allowed either to marry or to raise children. These opinions, however, would be rejected, I think, by most philosophers, who would hold, on the contrary, that homosexuality is not morally wrong, and that homosexuals should be allowed both to marry, and to raise children. Assume, for the sake of the present discussion, that the latter views are correct. Then, as Philip Kitcher and others have noted, cloning would seem to be a promising method of providing a homosexual couple with children that they could raise, since, in the case of a gay couple, each child could be a clone of one person; in the case of a lesbian couple, every child could, in a sense, be biologically connected with both people:

> A lesbian couple wishes to have a child. Because they would like the child to be biologically connected to each of them, they request that a cell nucleus from one of them be inserted into an egg from the other, and that the embryo be implanted in the uterus of the woman who donated the egg.[13]

Cloning to Save Lives

A final possibility is suggested by the well-known case of the Ayala parents in California, who decided to have another child in the hope, which turned out to be justified, that the resulting child would be able to donate bone marrow for a transplant operation that would save the life of their teenage daughter, who was suffering from leukemia. If cloning had been possible at the time, a course of action would have been available to them that, unlike having another child in the normal way, would not have been chancy: If they could have cloned the child who was ill, a tissue match would have been certain.

Objections to the Cloning of Humans

The Cloning of Mindless Organ Banks

Certain objections to the cloning of humans to produce mindless human organisms that would serve as a source of organs for others are perfectly intelligible. If someone objects to this idea on the grounds that one is destroying a person, the concern that is being expressed here is both completely clear and serious. The same is true if the objection is, instead, that such cloning is seriously wrong, since, in preventing a human organism from developing a functioning brain, one is depriving an immaterial soul associated with the organism in question of the possibility of experiencing life in this world. And, finally, the same is also true if someone holds that such cloning would be wrong, because it involves the destruction of an active potentiality for personhood.

The problem with these objections, accordingly, is not that they are in any way incoherent. Nor is it the case that the points raised are unimportant. The problem is simply that all of these objections are, in the end, unsound, for reasons that emerged earlier. Thus, the problem with the first objection is that there are excellent reasons for holding that human embryos do not possess those capacities, such as the capacity for thought and self-consciousness, that something must have, at some point, if it is to be a person. The problem with the second objection is that there are strong reasons for holding that the ontological basis for the capacities involved in consciousness, self-consciousness, thought, and other mental processes resides in the human brain, and not in any immaterial soul. Finally, the problem with the third objection lies in the assumption that the destruction of an active potentiality for personhood is morally wrong, for that claim is, on the one hand, unsupported by any satisfactory argument, and, on the other, exposed to decisive objections, one of which was set out earlier.

Often, however, it seems that people who would agree that the above objections are unsound, and who, moreover, do not view abortion as morally problematic, still express uneasiness about the idea of producing mindless human organ banks. Such uneasiness is rarely articulated, however, and it usually takes the form simply of describing the idea of mindless organ banks as a ghoulish scenario. This sort of dismissal of the use of cloning to produce organ banks is very puzzling. For what we are considering here is a way in which lives can be saved, and so, if one rejects this use of cloning, one is urging a course of action that will result in the deaths of innocent people. To do this on the grounds that mindless organ banks strike one as ghoulish seems morally irresponsible in the extreme: If this use of cloning is to be rejected, serious moral argument is called for.

The Cloning of Humans to Produce Persons

Violation of Rights Objections

Some people oppose cloning that is done with the goal of producing a person, on the grounds that such cloning involves a violation of some right of the person who is produced. The most important versions of this first sort of objection are those considered earlier, namely, that there is a violation either of a person's right to be a unique individual, or, more accurately, to be a genetically unique individual, or, alternatively, of a person's right to enjoy an open future that is not constrained by knowledge of the course of the life of some individual with the same genetic makeup. But for the reasons set out earlier, neither of these objections is sound.

Brave New World Style Objections

Next, there is a type of objection that is not frequently encountered in scholarly discussions, but which is rather common in the popular press, and which involves scenarios in which human beings are cloned in large numbers to serve as slaves, or as enthusiastic soldiers in a dictator's army. Such scenarios, however, do not seem very plausible. Is it really at all likely that, were cloning to become available, society would decide that its rejection of slavery had really been a mistake? Or that a dictator who was unable to conscript a satisfactory army from the existing citizens would be able to induce people to undertake a massive cloning program, in order that, 18 years or so down the line, he would finally have the army he had always wanted?

Psychological Distress

This objection is closely related to the earlier, violation of rights objections, because the idea is that, even if cloning does not violate a person's right to be a unique individual, or to have a unique genetic makeup, or to have an open and unconstrained future, nevertheless, people who are clones may feel that their uniqueness is compromised, or that their future is constrained, and this may cause substantial psychological harm and suffering.

There are two reasons for rejecting this objection as unsound. The first arises once one asks what one is to say about the beliefs in question, that is, the belief that one's uniqueness is compromised by the existence of a clone, and the belief that one's future is constrained if one has knowledge of the existence of a clone. Both beliefs are, as we have seen, false. But, in addition, it also seems clear that such beliefs would be, in general, irrational, since it is hard to see what grounds one could have for accepting either belief, other than something like genetic determinism, against which, as we saw earlier, there is conclusive evidence.

Once it is noted that the feelings that may give rise to psychological distress are irrational, one can appeal to the point that I made earlier, when we considered the question of whether knowledge of the existence of a clone might, for example, be damaging to one's sense of individuality, and whether, if this were so, such damage would be grounds for holding that there was a corresponding right that would be violated by cloning. What I argued at that point was that harm to an individual that arises because the individual has an irrational belief has a different moral status from harm that is not dependent on the presence of an irrational belief, and that, in particular, the possibility of the former sort of harm should not be taken as morally constraining others. The responsibility for such harm should, instead, be assigned to the individual who has the irrational belief, and the only obligation that falls on others is to point out to the person in question why the belief is an irrational one.

The second reason why the present objection cannot be sustained is also connected with the fact that the feelings in question are irrational, since the irrationality of the feelings means that they would not be likely to persist for very long, once cloning had become a familiar occurrence. For example, suppose that John feels that he is no longer a unique individual, or that his future is constrained, given that he is a clone of some other individual. Mary may also be a clone of some individual, and she may point out to John that she is very different from the person with whom she is genetically identical, and that she has not been constrained by the way the other person lived her life. Will John then persist in his irrational belief? This does not really seem very likely. If so, any distress that is produced will not be such as is likely to persist for any significant period of time.

Failing to Treat Individuals as Ends in Themselves

A fourth objection is directed, not against the cloning of persons in general, but against certain cases, such as those in which parents clone a child who is suffering from some life-threatening condition, in order to produce another child who will be able to save the first child's life. The thrust of this objection is that such cases involve a failure to view individuals as ends in themselves. Thus Philip Kitcher, referring to such cases, says that "a lingering concern remains," and he goes on to ask whether such scenarios "can be reconciled with Kant's injunction to 'treat humanity, whether in your own person or in the person of another, always at the same time as an end and never simply as a means.'"[14]

What is one to say about this objection? It may be important to be explicit about what sacrifices the child who is being produced is going to have to make to save his or her sibling. When I set out this sort of case under the subheading "Cloning to Save Lives," I assumed that what was involved was a bone marrow transplant. Kitcher, in his formulation, assumes that it will be a kidney transplant. I think that one might well be inclined to take different views of these two cases, given that, in the kidney donation case, but not the bone marrow case, the donor is making a sacrifice that may have unhappy consequences for that person in the future.

To avoid this complicating factor, let us concentrate, then, on the bone marrow case. In such a case, would there be a violation of Kant's injunction? There could be, if the parents were to abandon, or not really to care for the one child, once he or she had provided bone marrow to save the life of the other child. But this, surely, would be a very unlikely occurrence. After all, the history of the human race is mostly the history of unplanned children, often born into situations in which the parents were anything but well off, and yet, typically, those children were deeply loved by their parents.

In short, though this sort of case is, by hypothesis, one in which the parents decide to have a child with a goal in mind that has nothing to do with the well being of that child, this is no reason for supposing that they are therefore likely to treat that child merely as a means, and not also as an end in itself. Indeed, surely there is good reason to think, on the contrary, that such a child will be raised in no less loving a way than is normally the case.

Interfering with Personal Autonomy

The final objection that I shall consider is also one that has been advanced by Philip Kitcher, and he puts it as follows: "If the cloning of human beings is undertaken in the hope of generating a particular kind of person, then cloning is morally repugnant. The repugnance arises not because cloning involves biological tinkering but because it interferes with human autonomy."[15]

This objection would not apply to all of the cases that I mentioned in "Considerations in Support of the Cloning of Persons" as ones in which the cloning of a person would be justified. It does, however, apply to many of them. Is the objection sound? I cannot see that it is. First, notice that, in some cases, when one's goal is to produce "a particular kind of person," what one is aiming at is simply a person who will have certain potentialities. Parents might, for example, want to have children who are capable of enjoying intellectual pursuits. The possession of the relevant capacities does not force the children to spend their lives engaged in such pursuits, and so it is hard to see how cloning that is directed at that goal would interfere with human autonomy.

Second, consider cases in which the goal is not to produce a person who will be *capable* of doing a wider range of things, but an individual who will be *disposed* in certain directions. Perhaps it is this sort of case that Kitcher has in mind when he speaks of interfering with human autonomy. But is it really morally problematic to attempt to create persons who will be disposed in certain directions, and not in others? To answer this question, one needs to consider concrete cases, such as the sorts of cases that I mentioned earlier. Is it morally wrong, for example, to attempt to produce, via cloning, individuals who will, because of their genetic makeup, be disposed not to suffer from conditions that may cause considerable pain, such as arthritis, or from life-threatening diseases, such as cancer, high blood pressure, strokes, and heart attacks? Or to attempt to produce individuals who will have a cheerful temperament, or who will not be disposed to depression, to anxiety, to schizophrenia, or to Alzheimer's disease?

It seems unlikely that Kitcher, or others, would want to say that attempting to produce individuals who will be constitutionally disposed in the ways just indicated is a case of interfering with human autonomy. But then, what are the traits that are such that attempting to create a person with those traits is a case of interfering with human autonomy? Perhaps Kitcher, when he speaks about creating a particular kind of person, is thinking not just of any properties that persons have, but, more narrowly, of such things as personality traits, or traits of character, or having certain interests? But again one can ask whether there is anything morally problematic about attempting to create persons with such properties. Some personality traits are desirable, and parents typically encourage their children to develop those traits. Some character traits are virtues, and others are vices, and both parents and society attempt to encourage the acquisition of the former, and to discourage the acquisition of the latter. Finally, many interests, such as music, art, mathematics, science, games, physical activities, can add greatly to the quality of one's life, and once again, parents typically expose their children to relevant activities, and help their children to achieve levels of proficiency that will enable them to enjoy those pursuits.

The upshot is that, if cloning that aimed at producing people who would be more likely to possess various personality traits, or traits of character, or who would be more likely to have certain interests, was wrong because it was a case of interfering with personal autonomy, then the childrearing practices of almost all parents would stand condemned on precisely the same grounds. But such a claim, surely, is deeply counterintuitive.

In addition, however, one need not rest content with an appeal to intuitions here. The same conclusion follows on many high-order moral theories. Suppose, for example, that one is once again behind the Rawlsian veil of ignorance, and that one is deciding among societies that differ regarding their approaches to the rearing of children. Would it be rational to choose a society in which parents did not attempt to encourage their children to develop personality traits that would contribute to the latters' happiness? Or a society in which parents did not attempt to instill in their children a disposition to act in ways that are morally right? Or one in which parents made no attempt to develop various interests in their children? It is, I suggest, hard to see how such a choice could be a rational one, given that one would be opting, it would seem, for a society in which one would be likely to have a life that, on average, would be less worth living.

I conclude, therefore, that, contrary to what Philip Kitcher has claimed, it is not true that most cloning scenarios are morally repugnant, and that, in particular, there is, in general, nothing morally problematic about aiming at creating a child with specific attributes.

Conclusion

In this essay, I have distinguished between two very different cases involving the cloning of a human being—one that aims at the production of mindless human organisms that are to serve as organ banks for the people who are cloned, and another that aims at the creation of persons. Regarding the former, the objections that can be advanced are just the objections that can be directed against abortion, and, for reasons that I briefly outlined above, those objections can be shown to be unsound.

Very different objections arise in the case of cloning whose aim is the production of persons. Concerning this second sort of cloning, I argued that it is important to distinguish between the question of whether such cloning is, in principle, morally acceptable, and whether it is acceptable at the present time. Regarding the latter question, I argued that the present use of cloning to produce persons would be morally problematic. By contrast, concerning the question of whether such cloning is in principle morally acceptable, I argued, first, that such cloning is not intrinsically wrong; second, that there are a number of reasons why the cloning of persons would be desirable; and, third, that the objections that have been directed against such cloning cannot be sustained.

My overall conclusion, in short, is that the cloning of human beings, both to produce mindless organ banks, and to produce persons, is both morally acceptable, in principle, and potentially very beneficial for society.

Notes and References

[1]Donceel, J. F. (1970) Immediate animation and delayed hominization. *Theological Stud.* **31,** 76–105. Donceel refers to Rahner, K. (1967) *Schriften zur Theologie* **8,** 287.

[2]*See*, for example, Matthew 7:13–14 and 22:13–14.

[3]Di Berardino, M. A. and McKinnell, R. G. (1997) Backward compatible. *The Sciences* **37,** 32–37.

[4]Hart, R., Turturro, A., and Leakey, J. (1997) Born again. *The Sciences* **37,** 47–51.

[5]Brock, D. W. (1998) Cloning human beings: an assessment of the ethical issues pro and con, in *Clones and Clones*, Nussbaum, M. C. and Sunstein, C. R., eds., Norton, New York. *See* the section entitled "Would the use of human cloning violate important human rights?"

[6]Bouchard, T. J., Jr. (1997) Whenever the twain shall meet. *The Sciences* **37,** 52–57.

[7]Brock, D. in the section entitled "Would the use of human cloning violate important human rights?"

[8]Feinberg, J. (1980) The child's right to an open future, in *Whose Child? Children's Rights, Parental Authority, and State Power*, Aiken, W. and LaFollette, H., eds., Rowan and Littlefield, Totowa, NJ.

[9]Jonas, H. (1974) *Philosophical Essay: From Ancient Creed to Technological Man,* Prentice-Hall, Englewood Cliffs, NJ.

[10]*See*, for example, the discussion of this issue in Bouchard, pp. 55,56.
[11]Brock, D., in the subsection entitled "Human cloning would be a new means to relieve the infertility some persons now experience."
[12]*Ibid.*
[13]Kitcher, P. (1998) Whose self is it, anyway? *The Sciences* **37,** 58–62. It should be noted that, although Kitcher mentions this idea as initially attractive, in the end he concludes that it is problematic, for a reason that will be considered in the subsection "The Cloning of Humans to Produce Persons"
[14]*Ibid.*, p. 61.
[15]*Ibid.*, p. 61.

Bibliography

Bilger, B. (1997) Cell block. *The Sciences* **37,** 17–19.
Bouchard, T. J., Jr. (1997) Whenever the twain shall meet. *The Sciences* **37,** 52–57.
Brock, D. W. (1998) Cloning human beings: an assessment of the ethical issues pro and con, in *Clones and Clones*, Nussbaum, M. C. and Sunstein, C. R., eds., Norton, New York.
Callahan, D. (1993) Perspective on cloning: a threat to individual uniqueness. *Los Angeles Times*, November 12, B7.
Di Berardino, M. A., and McKinnell, R. G. (1997) Backward compatible. *The Sciences* **37,** 32–77.
Donceel, J. F. (1970) Immediate animation and delayed hominization. *Theological Stud.* **31,** 76–105.
Feinberg, J. (1980) The child's right to an open future. in *Whose Child? Children's Rights, Parental Authority, and State Power*, Aiken, W. and LaFollette, H., eds., Rowan and Littlefield, Totowa, NJ.
Fletcher, J. (1974) *The Ethics of Genetic Control,* Anchor Books, Garden City, NY.
Gurdon, J. B. (1997) The birth of cloning. *The Sciences* **37,** 26–31.
Hart, R., Turturro, A., and Leakey, J. (1997) Born again? *The Sciences* **37,** 47–51.
Jonas, H. (1974) *Philosophical Essay: From Ancient Creed to Technological Man* Prentice-Hall, Englewood Cliffs, NJ.
Kitcher, P. (1997) Whose self is it, anyway? *The Sciences* **37,** 58–62.

Macklin, R. (1994) Splitting embryos on the slippery slope: ethics and public policy. *Kennedy Inst. Ethics J.* **4,** 209–226.

Meade, H. M. (1997) Dairy gene. *The Sciences* **37,** 20–25.

Robertson, J. A. (1994) *Children of Choice: Freedom and the New Reproductive Technologies* Princeton University Press, Princeton, NJ.

Robertson, J. A. (1994) The question of human cloning. *Hastings Center Report* **24,** 6–14.

Wilmut, I. (1996) Sheep cloned by nuclear transfer from a cultured cell line. *Nature* **380,** 64–66.

Abstract

Although some scientists' public announcements of research tend to the hyperbolic, the recent success in cloning technology and its implications for the future have proven to be immensely significant for science, morality, and politics. Indeed, worldwide public reactions to the prospect of human cloning have been as fascinating as the science. This is evident from certain immediate responses to the President's National Bioethics Advisory Commission, in particular, by the self-described American Bioethics Advisory Commission, and from certain media reports. Both the science and the public responses are analyzed in relation to the long history of medical reflections and research relating to human life, which, it is suggested, needs careful study, and leads to reflections on nineteenth century science, to the earlier work of Francis Bacon, and in turn, to earlier historical ideas from ancient Greek physicians. The connections to in vitro fertilization and embryo transfer are especially relevant for the significant ethical issues, the public reactions to new technology, and the ambivalence in both public and professional literatures.

Surprise! You're Just Like Me!

Reflections on Cloning, Eugenics, and Other Utopias[1]

Richard M. Zaner[2]

The Wonder of It All

Not long ago, Walter Gilbert, a Nobel laureate in genetics, proclaimed with rare enthusiasm that the human genome now being unraveled, mapped, and sequenced in the National Institutes of Health's Human Genome Project,[3] and in laboratories around the world, promises to "put together a sequence that represents...the underlying human structure...our common humanity." Soon, he announced, it will be possible "to pull a CD out of one's pocket and say, 'Here is a human being; it's me'!"[4] Shortly after, equally stunning items have fairly blared from the pages of newspapers and from television screens, the most staggering doubtless being the success at animal cloning by the somatic cell nuclear transfer technique developed by Ian Wilmot, and the immediate implications for human cloning.[5]

Events such as these promise subsequent developments as stupendous and consequential as anything in human history. The wonder of it: There "I" would be, right on a CD, and you, there on that one. And none of the other, now passé notions filed away with so many others in that dusty room of human history should any longer pester or perplex us with curious, incomprehensible, often unpronounceable notions. Just stick that CD into a computer and, bingo, up "you" or "I" pop—supposing and hoping no ill-starred or inept mix-up has occurred!

Actually, Gilbert's image of the CD is itself somewhat dated, what with the wonders of biological miniaturization promising far more of such information on ever-smaller, tinier spots: All of it can, if you will, be biologized and digitalized, then dotted onto a minuscule chip (eventually a molecule), which itself could then be encrypted under a fingernail, or, more likely, into a more clandestine and unscannable place in the body. Obviously, as the promissory notes from the inevitable genome and cloning industries emerge, as they surely will, given the stunning prospects for knowledge and resulting technologies (not to mention the certain profits to be realized), the true marvel will not be far behind: allowing infertile people to select, from a shelf of made-to-order or standard-model embryos, just the baby they have long wanted. What once was consigned to the obscurity of science fiction is now daily grist for the mills of major media.

Another piece of this awesome prospect appeared in an article by one of the most respected minds in bioethics, Albert Jonsen. In it, he pins down what he regards as the real question at the heart of the Genome Project: "What constitutes the separateness that makes it possible to designate 'this person' and distinguish between 'this' and 'that' person?"[6] He is worried about what is heard so often when what used to be called the new genetics is discussed: How, in this bureaucratic world, can any of us keep information about ourselves from the prying eyes of people intent on getting such private data (Social Security numbers, bank account codes, charge card numbers, and so on)? Nor is it just insurance companies, employers, or government agencies who are busily engaged in keeping records of such information; the fact is that the utterly private and personal seems fair game for just about any business or individual with but modest computer skills and nothing better to do than poke their digitalized noses wherever they please.

If the question is what makes you and me different and separate, the problem, Jonsen avers, is privacy! Such familiar notions as appeals for confidentiality, informed consent, and disclosure of information that belongs to each individual only underscore the key place of privacy. Specifically, just as the legal right of self-determination is implied by the moral principle of autonomy, so is the right of privacy, which he believes is the moral fundament of the new genetics. Furthermore, at the core of privacy is the idea of "moral personhood:" Each individual has "a moral right to privacy because privacy is an acknowledgment of the moral personhood of each individual."[7]

Moral personhood is fundamental, for it constitutes "the core of my 'individual substance'."[8] Which brings Jonsen to an extraordinary claim: "My genome constitutes me," he says, for "at the core of my 'individual substance'" is a "repeated molecular structure that is mine alone," even though "much of that structure is the same in other individuals who have been generated by my ancestors and by my siblings."[9] So, the answer to the essential question is at hand: "What constitutes the separateness that makes it possible to designate 'this person' and distinguish between 'this' and 'that' person" is a "repeated molecular structure that is mine alone," yet sufficiently like what constitutes others as to make privacy concerns the primary ones.

The prospects of DNA testing or genetic screening turning into mere meddling makes privacy the prominent concern; as a moral right, it acknowledges each individual's moral personhood, which invokes the idea of individual substance, whose meaning or definition is in a genome that is not just genome, but allegedly somehow both me and mine. To express it the other way around: A molecular structure that is mine alone (but shared with many others in my kindred) both constitutes me and is mine, since it makes me this individual substance that is understood to have the privilege of being the moral right of privacy, since the individual is endowed with personhood, which, in the end, is the only true barrier to any of those nosy hackers (business or person) with nothing better to do than surf the web in search of what none have any right to without my permission and specific authorization.[10]

Since, of course, presumably the same must be said about any individual with its own genome—fetus, embryo, or zygote, and whether the individual is retarded, comatose, or whatever—then the same set of claims, about its being a me constituted by its genome and the like, would have to hold for each of these individuals—a proposal that seems at best quite odd. Unless, that is, such claims are supposed to hold only for sane, mature, rational individuals like Jonsen, you, and me, although this is not actually stated (which, obviously, raises some intriguing questions). What we might ask about this increasingly popular view is whether it does, in fact, deliver what it promises: "me"—all the more perplexing as human cloning advances, as it most surely will, ban or no ban.

Who am I? Am I my genes, or am I in my genes? In what sense, for that matter, might these genes, this genome, belong to me? Is what, at the nub of such things, separates thee from me found solely in the differences in the genome each of us respectively is or has? Either way—whether a matter of being or having—of course, then all the perennial passionate pursuits by so many driven philosophers must be shown the door. The answers, being the genes or in the genes, is not in any case in the quaint metaphysical quests that stirred the likes of Plato or Hegel, Kierkegaard or Kant, Aristotle or Dewey.

Something like full circle is then reached, for, in the days around the time of DNA's discovery—which *Life* magazine, in 1961, announced on its cover with only a modicum of hyperbole as the "secret of life," and which Kurt Vonnegut cut a literary jib about in his classic, *Cat's Cradle*—it was thought[11] that the new genetics was indeed, as Gilbert says, the holy grail, and the human genome the secret hiding place of self.

Will Wonders Never Cease?

We have been fairly inundated over the past few years with announcements directly from, or closely associated with, the genome project, for instance, that cloning of human cells, embryos, even individuals, has been going on, and, more recently, has been successful. Which raises intriguing questions: If a clone has, not almost the same, but by definition the very same molecular structure—the same DNA, genes, chromosomes, the works—what are we to think of Jonsen's or Gilbert's notions? Do I and a clone of me have the same genome? If so, what would there then be: me, so to speak, here in this body, and, at the same time, me over there in that body? But if I am, twisting things a bit, both here and there, if there is not one but two (or more) bodies, is it the same I? And, of the CD (or bio-chip) can we say, with Gilbert, "'Here is a human being; it's me'?" Is it that I am on (or in) the CD, or that I am—what? Am I the CD, or am I merely the digitalized markings or impressions on or in the CD? Moreover, since being on a CD would mean, I suppose, that any number of identical individuals (entities having or being the same genomic structure) can in principle be produced, of which can it be rightly said "it's me?" Does, can, or must each of the cloned individuals say, "It's me?" Am I all the individuals produced, or am I the master copy from which any and all such identical entities are produced? What can, do, should we make of all this? Am I my replicable genome or not? Does it, using Jonsen's vernacular, constitute me or not?

Such questions, however apparently exotic, are far from idle. Only a couple of years before Ian Wilmut cloned Dolly the sheep (utilizing the technique of nuclear transfer, hitherto not widely considered possible), another technique was reported by Jerry Hall and his team at George Washington University Medical School's in vitro fertilization laboratory.[12] In late 1993, Hall reported success with what he described as a more efficient embryological technique to assist infertile women achieve pregnancy. Immediately, a public furor erupted. *Time, Newsweek*, and other media worldwide, promptly announced that "cloning of human embryos" had arrived—with reactions and controversies, as fascinating as the research itself, rapidly appearing not only in the popular media, but also in the odd, but charming field, of bioethics. Responses to Wilmut's announcement were surprising only to the extent that they seemed oblivious of the public and scientific clamor provoked by Hall's announcement.

Cloning Rears Its Head

A taste of what was about to happen[13] was the spectacle of two seasoned contenders in bioethics battling it out in print, rather like a more somber obligato to the more raucous public chorus. John Robertson, obviously comfortable with the prospect of Hall's blastomere separation, took little time in embracing it as "ethically acceptable."[14] In a critical note accompanying Robertson's article, Richard McCormick expressed surprise at the "breathtaking...speed with which [Robertson] subordinates every consideration to its usefulness in overcoming infertility."[15]

Although allegedly merely trying to find a better way to resolve infertility—enabling the childless to conceive and bear children—Hall's aim was obfuscated by the ensuing media barrage insisting that, to the consternation of critics and delight of supporters, human embryos had truly been cloned. Now, after Wilmut's Dolly and Polly, can human cloning be far behind? Banned within the United States, of course, does not in the least mean that the effort will elsewhere be stopped in its tracks, which was dramatically demonstrated by Hall's and Wilmut's successes that typically conjured images of chimeras, golems, or monster dinosaurs cavorting about in some Jurassic park on the ready to devour, crush, or otherwise leave carnage behind.

Cloning, of course, occurs naturally in human beings, as identical twins, triplets, quadruplets, or the rarer birth of quintuplets. It has also been known for some time in animal and plant genetics; new individuals or strains having identical genetic makeups can be mass-produced by copying the DNA from dead (or live) wheat, corn, dinosaurs, mice, or cattle. Using Hall's method, an embryo at a very early stage of development (before cells have begun to specialize) is separated into as many as eight cells. DNA, extracted from each cell, is copied and transferred into unfertilized eggs, which are then grown into individual embryos, with each implanted in the uterus of a surrogate mother, giving rise to eight identical offspring, or clones.

Wilmot, on the other hand, accomplished true asexual reproduction. He demonstrated that the DNA in a cell nucleus taken from the udder of an adult ewe could, by depriving it of nutrition, be returned to the biological stage prior to specialization. After that, it could be inserted into another cell taken from another adult sheep, stripped of its nucleus, and, if the new cell was implanted into the uterus of a third adult female sheep, it would then grow into a new sheep. Strictly speaking, however, this would not be a cloned individual, since the mitochondria of the second cell makes its contribution, after all, yet Wilmot's technique was an extraordinary achievement.[16]

Although Hall denied, in 1993, that he had cloned human embryos, that is precisely what his team successfully did. Hall was eventually brought to admit that his research showed the possibility of doing in the laboratory what humans otherwise do naturally: test-tube twins or multiples. However, since nonviable embryos were used, Hall asserted that no ethical codes or norms had been violated; that would have been true, it was implied, only if viable embryos were used.[17]

In response to the public uproar, Hall stated that he had no plans to continue the research. Similarly, Wilmut's announcement was accompanied by a call for a world-wide ban on human cloning. Even so, both techniques are clearly crucial steps on the way to the stunning prospect of full human cloning. Several years ago, Robertson seemed to take particular delight in predicting that "the actual birth of children as a result of embryo splitting might well occur in the next two to five years."[18]

Public Reaction to Researchers: Can They Be Trusted?

The media have reported, and for the most part reacted negatively to, biomedical research findings, especially in genetics, that foreshadowed cloning—for a time after the Nuremberg medical trials in 1945–1946, briefly after Josuah Lederberg's praise in *The American Naturalist* of the increasing range of prospects from genetic engineering, especially the eugenic advantages (as he saw it) of human cloning, and several times after these events. As the National Bioethics Advisory Commission (NBAC) pointed out, Wilmot's cloning technique is merely "an extension of research that had been ongoing for over 40 years using nuclei derived from nonhuman embryonic and fetal cells."[19] Still, nothing quite matches the reactions to the announcements that occurred in 1993 and in 1997. Wilmut's press conference, in fact, was followed not merely by media outcries, but with actions in more than a dozen countries to ban or severely restrict human cloning by nuclear transfer.[20] Though perhaps only a momentary blip on the always dense screen of public opinion, the uproar in 1993 had one remarkable result: It was reported that Hall and his colleagues, voices "choking with emotion," recanted in an almost medieval way, proclaiming along the way their "deep reverence" for human life.

In a 1993 *New York Times* op-ed piece, Robert Pollack roundly declared that Hall's experiment "has brought us one step closer to Aldous Huxley's anti-utopian vision of mass-produced people."[21] The reports provoked any number of what-if scenarios,[22] and these continued to shudder into print after Wilmut's announcement.[23]

Such scenarios,[24] once regarded by most embryologists as highly fantastic, have become not only realistic, but veritable blue-prints[25] for scientific development. Even in early 1994, Robertson was inclined merely to add cloning "to the armamentarium of infertility treatment," and consoled critics that the likely uses of cloning techniques "are neither so harmful nor so novel" as to justify a ban, or even a moratorium[26]—a position he continued to take before the president's NBAC during its 1997 meetings on whether to ban human cloning in the United States.[27] Although differing from Robertson, Susan M. Wolf also regards the ban as unjustified.[28] On the other hand, McCormick's reply to Robertson was derisive: "If one has no ethical misgivings about cloning by blastomere separation, then John A. Robertson's essay should be a corrective."[29]

Where Will It End?

Scattered through the many books, articles, conferences, committees, and, more recently, the NBAC report, all trying desperately yet earnestly to promulgate coherent policies, is a fundamental rift between two views, each with its own assumptions, reasons, and conclusions, and neither having much to do with the other, except periodic indulgence in condemnation. On the one hand are those who praise the enhanced range of practical options for combating infertility and genetic diseases on the immediate horizon. All that is needed is a modest revision of the usual morality of autonomy, beneficence, and nonmaleificence, for who would dare deny the enormous potential for benefit of relief from the horrors of Alzheimer's, Tay-Sachs, cystic fibrosis, other diseases, or the indignity and frustration of infertility? What will ultimately justify all the effort and expense, and settle the contentious disputes is, not to put too fine a point on it, the payoff in the eventual forms of knowledge of life before birth, and, eventually, treatments to help stay the ravages of many diseases and depressing conditions—clearly an echo of Bacon's stern admonition that, unlike mere philosophy, knowledge must be put to the hard task of resolving the brute conditions of human life.

On the other hand, scholars such as McCormick, Paul Ramsey,[30] Kurt Bayertz,[31] Leon Kass,[32] and Hans Jonas[33] are far less optimistic. Jonas emphasized years ago that the prospect of genetic control, through cloning and other means, "raises ethical questions of a wholly new kind," for which we are profoundly unprepared. "Since no less than the very nature and image of man are at issue, prudence becomes itself our first ethical duty, and hypothetical reasoning our first responsibility."[34] Tinkering with traditional ethical norms is not sufficient for the new task created by the prospects of genetic control, and not sufficient to address the profound and altogether new ethical, existential, even metaphysical, issues inherent to the new genetics. For that, we must radically question genetic science and technology; indeed, the very foundations of moral life must be rethought.[35] Battle lines tend to be drawn very quickly; the times are fig-ripe for the sting of severe disputes that often erupt into literal violence, in many cases, apparently provoked by the prospects and by media announcements. Is it defensible in any sense, for instance, to set out forthwith to create "grade A individuals",[36] "kids made to order,"[37] whether designed as privileged deciders of policy or merely dumb drones for the duller humdrum chores of life? Since patenting of new life forms was legally endorsed the early 1980s, and because such made-to-order, cloned human cells, embryos, and even individuals quite obviously are new, and are life forms, are these next for patenting? Will it come to pass, as it were, that some people, perhaps even corporations, will own other people, as is now the case for cell-lines, laboratory animals, and strains of vegetables?

Alongside much conceptual, not to say emotional, confusion many people in our society manifest a marked ambivalence toward biomedical technologies—bewildered yet confident, enthralled yet panicky. Will we be any better off giving biomedical research free reign, or is it the wiser course to restrict or even ban certain types of research (human cloning, specifically, at least thus far)? Such a ban is ill-advised, as it would invariably involve "intruding into labs and monitoring the 'intent' of scientists."[38] Not mentioned in any of these discussions, it might be noted in passing, is whether or not the ban imposed could reasonably be understood as a violation of the First Amendment: Is scientific research, especially the current investigations into human cloning, a form of protected speech? The question has been raised from time to time about research, but little clarity has yet to be won, especially for legal purposes.[39]

"A fateful decision is at hand," Leon Kass wrote soon after the president accepted NBAC's recommended five-year moratorium on cloning: "To clone or not to clone a human being is no longer an academic question."[40] The moratorium, Kass and his colleagues on the ABAC contend, is merely the usual camel's nose under the tent: The NABC fully endorsed the value of cloning, not only of animals, but of human embryos as well, in order that safety matters can be appropriately determined. The members of ABAC, however, fully expect the ban to be lifted in the near future, unless it is made absolute, permanent, and international. Daniel Callahan, too, is troubled, seeing in the work of the NBAC a mere "minimalist ethic,"[41] its concern for safety mere patina against the march toward human cloning. NBAC's central concern for safety, however, James Childress insists, indicates the serious need for a window of opportunity to allow scientists to determine "whether safe human cloning would have unacceptable moral costs."[42]

An Accouchement of Clones: Breeding Chimeras?

Such conflicts are not new; in fact, most of the major issues in dispute were already evident at the beginning of the in vitro fertilization (IVF) debate decades ago. Much of the turbulence was also present regarding genetics, which was the very issue that brought Kass into the debate some years ago. It has often been pointed out that genetics and IVF (along with other so-called alternative means to achieve pregnancy) are of a piece. It is, in any event, clear from discussions over the past two or three decades that most research into life prior to birth, from the very earliest stages up to birth, is fraught with many of the same prickly questions. The current hostilities, and much of the same sorts of concern, over human cloning can be found, in fact, throughout the recent history of discussions over embryo research, abortion, selective termination, even *in utero* fetal surgical protocols, especially IVF.[43]

When infertility was interpreted as a disease, and thus as falling within the purview of medicine, for example, IVF swiftly became a growth industry for the new, supposedly medical treatment.[44] Then, as now, questions of both regulation and rationale were immediately raised, and came to as little then as may well happen now. Indeed, IVF became a veritable growth industry with astonishing speed, from two programs in 1981[45] to hundreds within a few years, and with hardly more than token regulation, despite well-publicized instances of abuse. Moreover, questions about the rationale for IVF were just as swiftly raised: What is it supposed to treat? Despite the physician-friendly language, Paul Ramsey, already in the early 1970s, had doubts about the very idea of conceiving infertility in this way, and issued a stern warning that IVF is but "manufacture by biological technology, not medicine."[46] Others, too, were dubious: what is supposedly treated is not a disease, but merely parental wishes. IVF was seen as an illicit extension of medicine that sinks us into a quicksand of "ethical relativism."[47] That parents may feel deeply about having children does not make these, or other, feelings appropriate objects of medical attention.

Quite reasonably, moreover, questions about IVF were seen as closely associated with equally serious issues raised by the new genetics. In her 1977 study, for instance, June Goodfield was vexed about three concerns she thought implicit to genetics: a slow erosion of what makes us uniquely human, an assault on personal autonomy and integrity, and a loss of control over the conduct and direction of human affairs.[48] Shortly after that, the physician-researcher, Gerald Weissmann, lamented that such critics are simply ignorant of science and its technological payoffs. He harshly rejected her anxieties as plays on popular superstitions that merely indulge the always-eager harbingers of doom and gloom: Her first worry is simply an expression of the fear of creating human beings by cabalistic rites (golems); the second restates the chimera myth; and the third confuses *Brave New World* with *The Double Helix*.[49] Readily detectable beneath the façade of criticisms such as Goodfield's, he argues, is in reality the specter of censorship.[50]

For that matter, Weissmann wrote, the question of ends has already been effectively settled. Although, he notes, there has been some skepticism about the usefulness of scientific knowledge, especially that which probes living things, not only is "there life in it yet," but in fact the bulk of it has yielded significant utilitarian benefit for society: studies into soil gave us streptomycin, cellular research resulted in the Salk vaccine, and studies of cell cycles in onion roots led to rational treatment for leukemia. For the scientist, that is, any residual doubts there may have been about the benefits issuing from experimental science have thus been well-resolved—the corollary to which is that "if [the scientist] performs his task professionally by doing *well*, he is doing *good*."[51] We can therefore concentrate on the means made available in the "toyshops of technology and the purses of our government,"[52] with a myriad of new drugs, anesthesias, surgical procedures, diagnostic wonders, and the like pouring out daily from a veritable cornucopia.

The single ethical stricture that governs biomedical science is, Weissmann believes, "Thou shalt not fudge the data."[53] Otherwise, scientific and medical morality are the same as society's: We "get not only the government, but the science, [we] deserve."[54]

The utilitarian values of the biomedical enterprise, as he argued, are a moral guarantee that scientific interventions into human life are intrinsically benign—even though he admits some problems have occurred whether society wanted it or not, mentioning the Hiroshima bomb, Auschwitz laboratories, and the psychiatry of the Gulag archipelago. He did not mention the other bomb, at Nagasaki, nor the numerous and deeply questionable radiation experiments conducted in the United States as part of officially condoned policy,[55] some of which were public knowledge even at the time he wrote, although, as a rheumatologist at New York University he would surely have known of many of these, as were the unethical experiments documented by Henry Beecher in 1966,[56] and the more than 200 by Henry Pappworth in 1968,[57] not to mention the thoroughly questionable adventure at Tuskegee.[58]

Medicine: The "Singular Art?"

We might well wonder, then, whether the ambivalence toward experimental science stems from a basic distrust of scientists (and their funders), or from what Weissmann and others lament is a basically antiscientific attitude, or even scientific illiteracy, widespread among nonscientists. However that may be, as already noted biomedical technologies, if not the basic science behind them, have long had a peculiar fascination in our society: We seem at once enchanted by, and fearful of, them. Why is this? Consider H. T. Engelhardt's words:

> Medicine is the most revolutionary of human technologies. It does not sculpt statues or paint paintings: it restructures man and man's life.... [It] is not merely a science, not merely a technology...[but is the] singular art...of remaking man, not in the image of nature, but in his own image....[59]

Hence, the more powerful medical science becomes, "the more able it is to remake man," and therefore the more necessary it is to "understand what medicine should do with its competence."[60] In a word, its toyshops make available powerful means to make "our human nature conform to our chosen goals."[61] The critical question is, he says (echoing Hans Jonas): Who decides which goals should be pursued? To which might be added: How are those who eventually decide to be selected?

Following the laboratory production of transgenic mice in 1980 by Frank Ruddle at Yale, and, about the same time, the embryo cloning of specially bred cattle, by the animal genetics program at the King Ranch and Texas A & M University, it had become altogether plausible to design and plan for the genetic manipulation and control of human life, individual and collective: If transgenic mice or cattle, why not transgenic humans? So pressing are such questions, Kurt Bayertz urged in agreement with Jonas, that a new discipline, genethics, has become imperative, because there is little in our traditional moral understanding or legal codes that is adequate to understand or even articulate the full ramifications of the new genetics. Nor is he alone, as even a modest scan of the burgeoning literature in genetics and alternative reproductive techniques makes plain.[62]

Furthermore, given the new, highly effective psycho-active drugs that have been in production for at least the past three decades, it has been plausible for some time to conceive, design blueprints for, and practice wholly novel forms of behavior and mind control over individuals, and even entire populations. What has occurred as a result is that wholly new content has been given to perennial issues such as self-awareness and freedom vs determinism, and has rendered present-day humanity a profound moral issue, perhaps making treasured notions like autonomy the stuff of nostalgia. To illustrate, I recall hearing about the discovery, in a major city in the western United States, of a source of natural lithium in the city's water supply—thereby accounting for the statistically significant lower amount of mental illness there, compared to other similar urban areas—and wondering: Would anyone know whether some mind-altering drug had been put into their water supply? Could the people downwind from the CIA's release of LSD into New York City's subway tunnels know what had hit them, much less why, or even that their mentation had become altered?

Beyond this, death itself is now often medically interpreted, at least in some circles, as little more than a genetic error in the body's somatic cells—a disease in that sense, susceptible therefore of being forestalled or even prevented. Not surprisingly, there are already blueprints afoot to bring human mortality under control, making death and the extension of life-span serious and heady issues.

That these were not fanciful notions even by the late 1970s may be judged from the writings of two Nobel laureates in the field. In his 1978 Gifford Lectures, for instance, brain specialist Sir John Eccles, long centrally concerned with the physiology of self and self-consciousness,[63] triumphantly declared that "planned genetic manipulation" will supersede the otherwise essentially chancy "natural process of biological mutation," and urged that new genetic techniques be used to "enslave" biological (including human) evolution, making animal and human species "more useful for exploitation"[64]—an all-the-more-plausible notion today, of course. Eccles was picking up on a proposal that has played a central role in Western societies for more than a century: that controlled human breeding should be undertaken, in particular by restricting the reproductive capacities of what many 19th century writers regarded as the dregs of humanity—the feebleminded, syphilitic, weak, disadvantaged, and poor, all of whom had hitherto been allowed, even encouraged, to reproduce ad nauseam, and who seriously threaten to undermine the quality and integrity of humanity,[65] acting contrary to the nature of natural evolution.

At about the same time as Eccles wrote, the Australian geneticist, Sir Macfarlane Burnett, argued that disease, physical injury, malnutrition, and every "critical matter" in human life are "wholly dependent" on our genes. It is, accordingly, to genetics that even the lowliest clinician will soon have to learn to turn in combating disease, and, in doing so, will fulfill the promise trumpeted in clarion notes over five centuries ago by Francis Bacon. "Here, if anywhere," Burnett asserted about each human being's genetic constitution, even "a modern philosopher will be most likely to find his approach to the problem of evil in the world. We may find in the end that war and evil, pain and disease, aging and death were inevitable as soon as a working pattern of life...had been devised."[66]

It was thus hardly surprising that psychologist Kenneth B. Clark was vigorously arguing, at about the same time, that if society's authorities want to combat human violence then behavioral scientists must be allowed, even encouraged, to use pharmacological substances. These sciences "are now the critical [ones]; they will determine the answer to the ultimate moral question of human survival."[67] In order to "stabilize and make dominant...[the] moral propensities" needed to control hostility and violence, he unblushingly proposed experiments, using target subjects, that would doubtless continue to win considerable favor today: The experiments were to be on "compulsive criminals," in order to determine the most effective and "precise forms of intervention and moral control of human behavior."[68] He regarded these experiments as obviously morally justified—a theme echoed in more recent, rather controversial conferences on the genetics of crime.

All of which ineluctably evokes those horror stories about genetics, and the slippery slopes connected to them, of which many of us have become so fond. Indeed, the stories acquire quite a bit more bite than they may otherwise be thought to have today, now that actual cloning of mammals has been achieved, and human cloning is both realistic and likely to occur before long. Medicine and biomedical science provide powerful means for ensuring that at least some people will conform, at least to someone else's sense of norms; the phantasmal images of the ease with which an entire city's water or air could be affected can hardly be lightly dismissed; this reality of which was brought rudely home on the occasion of the Japanese cult's diffusing nerve gas in Tokyo not long ago.

As Eccles said, for the first time in human history evolution not only can but should be controlled—by whom not being a question he presumably wished to pursue at the time, however. The kind of proposal Eccles made, among other things, signifies, Burnett was quick to emphasize, that most if not all the perennial puzzles that have long plagued philosophers, theologians, and the rest of us have now been, or soon will be, answered by the new genetics: death, disease, violence, evil and, presumably, life, peace, and justice as well. Proposals like Clark's, which closely conform to the long-enduring idea of eugenic prevention, improvement, and breeding,[69] to harness if not nullify stupidity, violence, and other disagreeable traits—still make good sense to many people, and indeed fit rather well today with the prevailing winds of much public and scientific opinion.

Francis Bacon: The Paradoxical Question of Ends

Such ideas are deeply rooted in Western history, especially since the advent of science in its specifically modern character.[70] The core views of biomedical scientists like Herbert Muller, Joshua Lederberg, Eccles, Gilbert, and others were already implicit in Francis Bacon's call for a new science. The cardinal point of his "general admonition to all," was most clearly expressed by Bacon in his *The Great Instauration*: the deep affinity, as it might be termed, between theory and practice. To subdue and alleviate the "necessities and miseries of humanity," "a line and race of inventions" (that is, technologies) is needed. For that battle on behalf of humanity, then, "those twin objects, *human knowledge* and *human power,*" must come together "for the benefit and use of life."[71] However, understanding that thus understood, knowledge and its inventions are essentially defined by the uses to which they are put, and that these uses can be for ill or good, Bacon insisted that "charity and benevolence" are needed to govern our uses of knowledge and inventions.

Yet, since theory, in Bacon's radically new sense, Jonas points out, can say nothing about the ends to which knowledge and its inventions are put, a crucial and irresolvable paradox is, by that very fact generated. From whence, after all, can we, scientists or laypersons, learn what charity and benevolence are, much less how to incorporate them in our lives? In Jonas's words, "charity [or benevolence] is not itself among the fruits of theory in the modern sense." Even more, he points out,

> modern theory is not self-sufficiently the source of the human quality that makes it beneficial. That its results are detachable from it and handed over for use to those who had no part in the theoretical process is only one aspect of the matter. The scientist himself is by his science no more qualified than others to discern, nor even is he more disposed to care for, the good of mankind. Benevolence must be called in from the outside to supplement the knowledge acquired through theory: it does not flow from theory itself.[72]

Bacon was, in part, contending with the classical view of theory as contemplation, which he regarded as the "boyhood of knowledge": "It can talk, but it cannot generate; for it is fruitful of controversies but barren of works." It is the realm of the changeable and variable, or, as Jonas says, the commonplace, that must be known, and, in this vision of the new sciences, "to know" comes to mean[73] "to gain control" over things that are known simply because they are known. The whole point of knowledge is to give knowers the ability to overcome human misery, which was a driving and compelling force quite obviously at work in the Hall experiment, even more so in Wilmut's announcement, as well as throughout the Human Genome Initiative. For that preeminently practical task, science and nature must be conceived in terms of power. Jonas's interpretation then follows naturally: that such practical use is by no means accidental to modern science and theory more generally; it is, indeed, integral to it. In different words, Jonas contends, "The fusion of theory and practice becomes inseparable in ways which the mere terms 'pure' and 'applied' science fail to convey. Effecting changes in nature as a means and as a result of knowing it are inextricably interlocked:" science is technological by its nature.[74]

As noted already, Bacon himself realized that, since power can be used for evil as well as for good, science must be governed by charity and benevolence. Use is always, he knew, for something, it designates the means designed to bring about some end. For Bacon, the end is the betterment and preservation of human life—a goal which, it bears emphasis, was not itself justifiable in Bacon's work. In the classical thought of Plato and Aristotle, on the other hand, the benefit of genuine knowledge came precisely and only to those actually engaged in the pursuit of understanding, and the good was considered the essential goal of all efforts to know: the being of the knower undergoes transformation by the very seeking to know, but what is known remains unaltered by that—precisely the reverse of that pressed by Bacon. For him and modern science generally, knowledge is not the source of the human quality that makes it beneficial. Here, Weissmann seems far closer to understanding the character of modern theory than Goodfield; the question, however, is: From whence does that supplement flow?

However odd, the underlying thesis in the Baconian understanding of knowledge and its relation to practice is the same as can be found in many discussions today of the ethical dimensions of medicine and biomedicine: The idea that if something works, and is in that way useful, it must also be ethically acceptable. The response to which is, quite simply, that this begs the crucial ethical question, since usefulness cannot itself be what makes infertility, cloning, or anything else ethically acceptable.

The oddity was nestled deep in the heart of Bacon's vision: Neither the pursuit nor the acquisition of knowledge (science) are the sources of what makes them good or beneficial; this must rather be called in from outside (as Weissmann noted). And this leaves us utterly in the dark: For something to be useful means that it is useful for something; to say that something works, means that it works toward or for some goal or end. But with science posited as the sole meaning of knowledge in the Baconian world, we neither know what charity and benevolence are, nor how best to govern the uses of our inventions wisely. The very terms of this epistemological vision (clearly in the writings of Weissmann, Eccles, Burnett, Gilbert, and others) signify that neither charity and benevolence nor other virtues can possibly themselves be known at all, or, if known in some way, known in the same way that other things are known; nor are they fruits of that knowledge. So how can we know, and more significantly perhaps, become benevolent and charitable?

Yet knowing and being good are, Bacon insisted, essential to knowledge or theory; they must be governed in charity and benevolence. Yet Bacon was right: Even though they are incomprehensible by his theory—conceived as married to power—the very idea of power demands that charity and benevolence somehow come to govern that use.

The acute paradox inherent to modern science and medicine, so understood, is clear. In Jonas's direct terms, "the use of theory does not itself permit of a theory: if it is enlightened use, it receives its light from deliberation which may or may not enjoy the benefits of good sense."[75] What about this knowledge of use? How and where is that learned? In the Baconian scheme of things, it is not only utterly different from the knowledge of the theory used, but is essentially different from any theory at all. We can never acquire understanding of the good, then, from science or its inventions. For the modern understanding, Jonas therefore concluded, "there is theory and use of theory, but no theory of the use of theory."[76]

Nor is Bacon's call for a "race of inventions" to alleviate the miseries of humanity altogether novel. Already in classical Greek times, after all, there was a kind of celebration of human powers and interventions into the cosmic order of things. In medicine, this was also well known: Everything taken into the body, it was thought, had its impact on the soul; hence, through dietetics, one could, in principle, either correct the effects of bad diet (one of the main ways illness was understood) or bring about certain effects by means of a proper diet. Galen knew this quite well, and believed that dietetics could elevate and improve human beings far more effectively than any form of moral training. As Oswei Tempkin expressed the point in his interpretation of Galen, medicine (in its dietetic form accepted by Galen) includes an inherent moral aspect, in that Galen interpreted most diseases as caused by errors of regimen (thus, as avoidable); accordingly, health "becomes a responsibility and disease a matter for possible moral reflection." It is but a step from this to Galen's more direct declaration that medicine itself must come to "elevate man beyond the possibilities of purely moral teaching."[77] As such, there is introduced into medical history a crucial theme, that medicine itself must be construed as a device to improve man beyond what is possible from mere philosophy. Eugenic ideas are a deep part of our social and medical, and not only our scientific, history.

Still, it seems no exaggeration to note that with modern technology, which developed direct from the Baconian marriage of knowledge and power, everything radically changes. Jonas later noted that there is a "critical *vulnerability* of nature to man's technological intervention—unsuspected before it began to show itself in damage already done,"[78] which is evident in the sheer scale and speed of current technological invasions. Of more immediate import today, of course, are the prospects of genetic research and its many promised interventions: rectifying the ravages of genetic diseases, enhancing the quality of life for future generations, controlling violent behavior, and even altering our sense of death, and therefore life. From whence the charity and benevolence to govern these uses?

Clearly, modern technology has brought profound and lasting changes in its wake, giving real weight to Engelhardt's idea that medicine is the "singular art" of remaking the human estate, individually, and collectively. Not only a science or an art, but, as the father of modern pathology, Rudolph Virchow, remarked, medicine is a social science in its very bone and marrow. With contraception, genetic manipulation, in vitro fertilization, organ transplantation, massive inoculation programs, blastomere separation and cloning, and even cosmetic surgery, medicine is clearly an active agent of individual and social change.

All of which invokes fundamental ethical issues that are at the heart of medicine and biomedical research. Although infrequently, if ever, at the top of current social or scientific agendas, the keen paradox in Bacon's appeal for charity and benevolence remains, however, not as merely outside, but within. Medicine remakes our individual and social lives, but for the most part its governing values, even its vaunted, if at times disingenuous, commitment to truth ("Thou shalt not fudge the data," Weissmann says), have rarely been explicit.

The hard issue, in Engelhardt's words, is to discover "proportion and measure so that its Promethean endeavor can be undertaken without the hubris which invites tragedy.... Man has become more technically adept than he is wise, and must now look for the wisdom to use that knowledge he possesses."[79] But is there any such wisdom, and where might it be found? It may be well to recall T. S. Eliot's incisive questions: Where is the knowledge we have lost in information, where the wisdom we have lost in knowledge? Keen barbs, these, later echoed by Jonas:

> [We are] constantly confronted with issues whose positive choice requires supreme wisdom—an impossible situation for man in general, because he does not possess that wisdom, and in particular for contemporary man, who denies the very existence of its object: viz., objective value and truth. We need wisdom most when we believe in it least.[80]

From Galen to Darwin: Modern-Day Eugenics

Already evident in Bacon's work, and much subsequent scientific thinking, is the growing demand to combat the "miseries and necessities" endemic to the human condition (famine, epidemic, pestilence, and the like).

Bacon's call for a race of inventions to alleviate human misery is not, as noted, altogether novel. Jonas noted the "awestruck homage to man's powers" in classical times —a celebration of man's "violent and violating irruption into the cosmic order," although it had "a subdued and even anxious quality" about it. Despite a "restless cleverness" in human building, the encompassing character of nature and natural things is left unchanged and undiminished. "They last, while his schemes have their short-lived way."[81] Bayertz recalls, too, one of the earliest known "eugenic Utopias," Plato's *Republic* with its concern for "deliberately breeding human beings."[82] Moreover, as I have suggested elsewhere,[83] in one form or another this theme seems to have been a guiding motif in medicine at least since the appearance of dietetics in ancient Greece, and, as was noted earlier, clearly since Galen,[84] for whom health was a "responsibility and disease a matter for possible moral reflection," and medicine the means to "elevate man beyond the possibilities of purely moral teaching."[85] Thus, the idea of improving the human lot is quite as ancient as the effort to diagnose and heal.

Bayertz emphasizes that, until very recently, such eugenic conceptions, essentially extrapolations to human beings from plant and animal breeding, were merely playful musings with little lasting effect. By the late nineteenth century, however, it had become a widely embraced movement,[86] inspired in many ways by Darwin's biological understanding of human miseries and necessities. Key to the success of Darwin's theory and to later social Darwinism, was, Bayertz suggests, the pervasive mood of degeneration through much of the 1800s. The central notion behind this, and key to Darwin's understanding of evolution, was that, although the survival of the fittest is what drives the evolution of plants and animals, it obviously does not function in the same way in human life. This appeared to be particularly true for civilized human societies, in which the feeble in body and mind are not eliminated in the struggle to survive but, to the contrary, are actively supported, their struggle often abetted, and they are even encouraged to reproduce at will.

Darwin thus insisted, in 1871:

> With savages, the weak in body or mind are soon eliminated; and those that survive commonly exhibit a vigorous state of health. We civilized men, on the other hand, do our utmost to check the process of elimination; we build asylums for the imbecile, the maimed, and the sick; we institute poor-laws; and our medical men exert their utmost skill to save the life of every one to the last moment.[87]

Since "the weak members of civilized societies [are encouraged to] propagate their kind," which is "highly injurious to the race of man," since it directly leads to the degeneration of "man himself,"[88] such individuals must be prevented from reproducing, as in fact they were, here and elsewhere, for decades. Thus, Bayertz points out,

> [I]f modern civilization strips natural selection of its powers, and if this causally leads to degeneration, then natural selection must be replaced by consciously controlled *artificial selection*...on the one hand, [by] excluding genetically "inferior" individuals from reproduction...and, on the other hand, by giving individuals with desirable characteristics the opportunity to have as many off-spring as possible.[89]

As was already noted, precisely this replacement of natural selection by consciously controlled artificial selection came to be expressly advocated by Sir John Eccles in his prestigious Gifford Lectures delivered in 1978. It is thus hardly surprising to find that the chief passion driving the Human Genome Project, especially by a public sometimes either skeptical or jaded, is to discover ways of controlling, curing, or ameliorating diseases.

Detailing this fascinating movement with its ardent convictions, later taken over by the Nazis, is beyond our scope here.[90]

Of immediate concern, rather, are certain of the underlying assumptions that gave life to those early (and later) eugenicists, and continues today, often more subtly, as one of the more prominent rationales not only of cloning, but also of the Genome Project.

Is Cloning Sinister or What?

If nothing else, we surely must be a good deal more candid than usual when thinking about matters with the magnitude cloning harbors for society, especially given the continuing fury of the disputes over the past several decades, and ongoing today. Why does cloning disturb so many people?

Cloning, Like IVF, Implies that People Want Perfect Babies, Right?

And, although it may be laudatory to seek perfection, it is most often regarded as plain hubris, and unjustified. One would think, though, that the prospect of being able to cancel or ameliorate the effects of genetic diseases and crippling defects would be widely praised, celebrated with loud applause—and, of course, funded. Surely, no sane and rational parent would deliberately wish on their children the devastation of Tay-Sachs, cystic fibrosis Alzheimer's, prostate cancer, polycystic kidney disease, or any other of the more than six thousand known hereditary diseases—not if something corrective could be done about them.

But, after the media blitz following Hall's experiments, and even more so after Wilmut's success at cloning Dolly, and, more recently, Polly, people publicly fretted aloud about sinister and nasty surprises concocted by sly, not altogether forthright scientists, and awaiting an unwary public, "as if," Barbara Ehrenreich acerbically remarked, "someone had proposed adding Satanism to the grade-school curriculum."[91] After Dolly, Polly, and other mammals cloned using Hall's technique, both popular media and professional literature were thick with tangible fears and anxieties. Not only, Kass lamented this past summer, do most people actively expect abuses and misuses by untrustworthy scientists and their funders, but "many people feel oppressed by the sense that there is probably nothing we can do to prevent it from happening."[92]

Those who spoke from religious concerns were hardly alone in expressing alarm and even panic about what many fervently believe is bound now to occur. During the quarrel about genetics in the mid-1970s, even the most secular of folks began throwing around notions of sanctity and dignity, and dredging up antique arguments attacking scientific hubris. Were critics saying that the mere attempt to conceive, bear, and rear disease-free children is something evil? Some promoted the notion that an infertile couple's pursuit of in vitro fertilization meant that they really wanted a perfect baby. But what is meant by the *perfect* baby? Is not every normal baby perfect, for its parents? And isn't health, surely at the start of life, a key ingredient of that, and does not and should not every parent fervently want that for each of their children, and do whatever it takes to ensure that, as much as humanly possible? If, as has now happened, women taking drugs when they become pregnant are later successfully sued in court for child abuse, should not the very same concern be applauded when it is a matter of manipulating the genetic code? Is not there more than a bit of hypocrisy in all that talk of perfect babies?

Property, the Right to Be Born, and the Right to Reproduce

It may in any event be too late to turn back from the slippery road we have been traveling for quite some time, a road well-paved by the ample cornucopia of technologies daily emerging from the toyshops of science. Recombinant DNA research resulted in new life forms (animals and plants), for instance, for which patents, some outrageously generous, were swiftly awarded for life forms that could then be bought, sold and traded like any other marketplace commodity. Since cloned human embryos are also life forms, indeed, potentially quite lucrative ones, are they not also commodities in precisely the same sense, and therefore able to be patented, bought, sold, or traded? Underlying this prospect is at least in part the notion that embryos (cloned, harvested, donated, and eventually patented) are property, quite as much as any other part of a person's holdings.

This very point, involving the disposition of frozen embryos, was urged several years ago in a Tennessee court case. After several attempts at in vitro fertilization and with seven cryopreserved embryos awaiting implantation, a couple divorced. The wife sought to keep control of the embryos for her own future use, but her former husband's challenge in court raised the question: Whose property are they? That is, who does, or should, retain decisional control over them? If, as was alleged by the initial judge in the case, these embryos had a right to be born, then should not the woman's wishes be respected, and the embryos awarded to her? But if so, how can her right and planned use be respected, when the husband, whose sperm had been used to fertilize those embryos, refused to become a father by any means involving the use of those embryos? Could the court gainsay his right to refuse? But if, as eventually occurred, the husband's right to *refuse* was acknowledged and accepted (and the embryos then destroyed), did not that decision compromise his former wife's right?

Beyond that, did not those embryos also have rights, and, since the father's rights were given precedent, were not the supposed rights (perhaps, civil rights) of the embryos, to be born, also violated? Was the recalcitrant prospective father, because of his decision about the embryos, also guilty of killing human life, perhaps even murder? Furthermore, if that is true (and the Tennessee Supreme Court did grant the father-husband decisional control), what of the countless ova from fetuses and cadavers, which, fertilized with human sperm from whatever source, is an untapped and virtually limitless supply that could be used to meet the demand of infertile couples?

Often accompanying such cases is an appeal to another supposed right. People turn to the in vitro industry in order to have children they otherwise cannot have. Do these women have a right to reproduce just as much as do fertile people? If so, on whom does the corresponding obligation fall? If this is a genuinely positive right, nothing should be allowed to interfere, neither infertility, monetary costs, nor squeamish feelings about embryos, fetuses, cadavers, or cloning.

Behind the continuing disputes are other assumptions that make such claims questionable. For instance, appealing to the wants or desires of infertile people may not by itself justify using technologies like IVF, because it does not seem altogether coherent to regard desires and feelings such as these as proper objects of medical attention.[93] Another underlying assumption is the target of Ehrenreich's caustic observation that "some people's genetic material is worth more than others' and deserves to be reproduced at any expense." Part of what is dubious here is not hard to find: the attraction and, increasingly, encouragement of alternative reproductive technologies—artificial insemination, surrogate mothering, IVF, and now cloning—is striking, even while the number of children living in poverty and without adequate health care or schooling has steadily risen over the past decade. Indeed, for all the current talk about improving the health care system, serious questions remain about how, or even whether, proposed new plans will cover such children adequately, or at all, especially any children resulting from genetic cloning, much less the results of the first attempts, at least some of which are bound to be failures in some sense.

A Slippery Slide from In Vitro to Eugenics?

Along with the slide from patenting new life forms to the potential for patenting cloned human tissues and organs, and eventually whole human beings, the marketing, selling, and buying of IVF have already met with solid social approval or, at the very least, indifference. But whether acceptance or acquiescence, we may surely wonder whether we have not thereby given up any right to complain about cloning, and, if so, can eugenics, the deliberate attempt to design and improve human beings, or so called positive eugenics, be far behind? As noted earlier, plans are already afoot for engaging in precisely this attempt.

It should be pointed out that, although IVF is among the direct ancestors of cloning, it is not the only precedent in a history that stretches back to developments in the 1950s, to sterilization laws, earlier (at the time, more acceptable) forms of eugenics, and to the earliest days of Western medicine, which was understood, well before Bacon's clarion call, as directly involved in improving the lot of human life, through dietetics, as Galen expressly emphasized in the second century.[94] The history of medicine is replete with subtle and unsubtle hints about improving the human lot.

In fact, the practice of IVF provides motivation enough for doing something more than merely harvesting and fertilizing eggs, then transferring resulting embryos to some natural or artificial uterus. It was realized very early by professionals in the field that, given the initially dismal rate of success at achieving pregnancy, the IVF technique had to be made more effective, if it were ever to become widely accepted and practiced.[95] Some of the first attempts involved the use of powerful hormones, so that the female partner would produce more eggs than normal, which could then be harvested at one time.

But hyperstimulation of the ovaries, it was clear early on, carries worrisome complications, such as severe mood swings, cramps, bloating, nausea, and lethargy. Eventually, these were sufficiently frequent as to constitute an ovarian hyperstimulation syndrome, which can also lead to acute fluid accumulation in the peritoneal, pleural and pericardial cavities, causing pulmonary distress, blood clots, and even death.[96] Indeed, women who become pregnant with these hormones have four times the normal incidence of ovarian cancer; those who do not get pregnant face the risk of ovarian cancer that is up to ten times the normal rate.[97] Since such drugs have systemic and long-lasting effects on women, it also seems reasonable to suspect that the uterine environment is also affected, even altered, and may have consequences for fetal development.

Just because these megadoses of hormones can be hazardous, time-consuming, and expensive, it was realized that another procedure might be preferable: cryopreservation. If more than one good egg can be retrieved at a single time, then used to fertilize more than one embryo, after all, why not freeze some of them so that neither the fertility risks (nor the indignities that male partners undergo) need to be repeated? Hall's venture into embryonic cloning clearly had precisely the same rationale: His technique would circumvent even more hazards, discomforts, and costs of the usual IVF. Similarly, Robertson has not unreasonably urged that cloning by nuclear transfer is quite clearly little more than a rational extension of the same rationales that fueled IVF from the beginning: the fervent desire to bear one's own children, and the equally strong aim to avoid unnecessary risks, costs, pain, and suffering.

There is thus a quite direct line from the beginning to the end, and internally from one stage to the next, and an almost undetectable step then to the bountiful prospects of genetics, cloning, even eugenics—a fine demonstration of a slippery slope, which, given how eagerly the desire to have and bear one's own infant is accepted and promoted in our society, may be just as upsetting as the rather fanciful speculations unsettling the sleep of "what-ifers." Indeed, is not the promise of being able to cancel the deleterious results of known genetic diseases and defects quite enough reason to proceed apace with such ventures?

If an existing child suffers from a disease whose treatment calls for a bone marrow transplant, and the best sample of that would come from a disease-free identical twin and initially frozen embryo (cloned or natural), would it not be good for parents to seek the transplant? Indeed, would not (and should not) they and their considerable exercise of courage be praised? Drugs, freezing, transplants of organs and tissues, after all, actually work. In the past few years, in fact, quite a few couples have produced babies to provide tissue, including bone marrow, for one of their existing children. Weissmann's and Robertson's views both imply, after all, that a utilitarian calculus of usefulness will justify precisely such adventures, and who are Kass or the American Life League's American Bioethics Advisory Commission (ABAC) to gainsay the positive moral character of that use, when children are in fact thereby helped?

But Won't Cloning Seriously Compromise Our Treasured Individuality?

Appealing to the cherished value our society attaches to unique individuality, some people apparently decry the prospect of a bunch of identical clones walking around with the rest of us. Would not a cloned kid feel existentially distraught if she learned that she is but one among hundreds of other kids who are just like her? Surprise! You're just like me!

The concern rings a bit hollow. A cloned child or two, Ehrenreich acidly remarks, would probably feel no worse, and might even feel better than the kid who right now is merely the "3 millionth 13-year-old dressed in identical baggy trousers, untied sneakers and baseball cap—a feeling usually described as 'cool.'"[98] In fact, it has frequently been observed[99] that being unique may be the source of more distress than being like others in a consumer society, where the "holy of holies...is the shop," not the temple.[100] It is probably not true that many of us believe—we may not even want to believe—that we are each unique, singular happenings in the billion-footed universe: What a breathtaking idea, and what awesome responsibility it harbors.

It takes no great predictive powers to realize that just as IVF quickly became socially acceptable, so in all likelihood will human cloning. Robertson clearly thinks so and has no problem with that, nor do many others, such as Childress, so long as the question of safety can be resolved. And, as with IVF, even if at first so costly that only the wealthiest could afford such biological techniques, products, and other gewgaws, their increasing social acceptance will doubtless result in decreasing costs, to the point at which even the more common folks could eventually have access. At that point, the very reasons people want to have and bear babies the natural way, and turn to infertility clinics when they cannot, might similarly fuel a cloning industry, as Kass fears, and questions about the replication of one's own genetic endowment would surely then arise when the easier, natural way is readily available, which, however, would surely not be the first time human beings have exhibited narcissism.

What about the fear that cloning will result in a fateful surfeit of subhumans—dumb drones designed for the coarse drudgery of daily life, or merely to gratify parental vanities? It should be pointed out that, in a sense, there is nothing new about these; it is not now uncommon for people to practice a human version of animal husbandry, doing what we can, crudely put, to breed children for looks, good lineage, and good chances in life, if not for future SAT or MCAT scores. Neither is it particularly novel for some people to use other people—legal and illegal immigrants, ghetto residents, children, and so on— for their own gratification or the more menial chores of the workaday world, with a status only barely distinguishable from any of the possible ways cloned drones might be treated.

In the end, were we to become serious about valuing each person's uniqueness, a number of current social practices would just have to go: sweatshops, child labor, and itinerant farm workers, not to mention slums, insurance redlining, and a lot more. Indeed, if these matters continue to be thought of in property terms, there would then be no good reason to distinguish cloned embryos from other forms of property: "It's hard to see why people should be able to sell their labor, for example, but not their embryos or eggs," Ehrenreich observed. Never forget, she continued, "Labor is also made out of the precious stuff of life—energy and cognition and so forth—which is hardly honored when 'unique individuals' by the millions are condemned to mind-killing, repetitive work,"[101] not to mention to starvation and the killing fields of Rwanda, Bosnia, Laos, Somalia, or the social tragedy of our own ghettos.

Whose Power, What Ends?

We remain deeply ambivalent about biomedical technologies: They provoke fear yet fascinate, in part, perhaps, because we who use them need neither knowledge or understanding: faucets, telephones, antibiotics, and the rest are useful, when they work, and we do not have to know why. Especially in the case of biomedical technologies is the charm clear: They are powerful means to make "our human nature conform to our chosen goals," as Engelhardt says, whether by curing, correcting, or ameliorating otherwise devastating diseases or injuries, or by frankly altering what we are and how we interrelate with each other, and for good or ill. If not on stage, Clark, Weissmann, Eccles, Burnett, and others eagerly await in the wings. Perhaps most of us realize that the question of chosen goals is unavoidable: everything in our lives moves toward some end, whether or not deliberately devised, understood, or in harmony with other cherished values.

Yet, the dilemma remains: We remain in the dark about the best ends, nor are we confident that any among us, singly or in concert on local IRBs or federal commissions, have the wit or wisdom to speak on our behalf or on that of chosen goals. Distrust is woven deep into our social fabric. The charm of technological means augurs fear about ends. The fierce reactions to the idea of cloning are surely understandable, whatever their source, whether asserting that human life is too precious to be trusted to the vested hands of scientists, or that the new genetics is but another sinister attempt by a corrupt government and its capitalist backers, driven by greed, to control everything, or that it all but guarantees dehumanization by some of others and ultimately of us all.

The perceptive words of the scholar, C. S. Lewis, are sobering: the promised power of the new genetics is, in fact, he recognized many years ago, "the power of earlier generations over later ones," but there are no guarantees about their wisdom, or lack of it. Our perfectly understandable fear of that power ultimately stems from the fact that it is "possessed by some men [sic] which they may, or may not, allow [others] to profit by."[102] Ehrenreich would emphatically agree, and doubtless would not be alone: What we should fear, she says, is not so much twenty-first-century technology as putting such powerful biological technologies into the hands of twentieth-century capitalists and scientists still under the sway of Bacon's vision.[103]

These disputes are hardly new, as was already evident at the beginning of the IVF debate decades ago. By interpreting infertility as a disease, and thus bringing it within the prevailing medical model, the IVF industry swiftly became pervaded with this medical treatment.[104] To this, Paul Ramsey retorted that IVF was little more than "manufacture by biological technology, not medicine."[105] What is treated is not a disease or injury, but merely parental feelings, H. O. Tiefel insisted, and putting these "shifting individual preferences" together with the "physician's desire for a perfect child," sinks us into a quicksand of ethical relativism to be avoided at all costs.[106]

Pandora's Box or Utopian Cornucopia?

For more than three decades, a highly animated and far-reaching dispute has been going on over the prospects and implications of the new genetics, all highlighted by the recent successes at blastomere separation and cloning from an adult cell. The dispute gained clear focus when James Watson led the fight for federal funding of the Human Genome Project, which Gilbert termed the holy grail of human biology. Cloning surely has figured as among the best candidates for that grail.

On the other hand, there is another core theme running throughout the long history of the eugenic idea, from the early hints in the Hippocratic corpus and Plato's *Republic* to the time when the genetic code was first cracked: in Bayertz's words, the "orientation of eugenic policies towards the practice of [human] breeding."[107] From the earliest inklings of the notion that what was learned from animal and plant breeding could be transferred to human populations, the dominating themes are, on the one hand, to correct the defects people suffer, and, on the other, to search for ways to improve human life, so that the propensity of civilized humanity to degeneracy can be stopped in its tracks: the latter a deeply ironic theme. Although the force driving people to favor genetics is probably negative eugenics (diagnosing and treating diseases), the motivation to positive eugenics has clearly been an accompanying, if most often unspoken, force from the beginning. These deep-seated motifs within Western society, medicine in particular, have at the same time regularly met with equally passionate opposition, usually in the form of religious and moral objections accompanied by a profound sense of doom if nature is given over carte blanche to human scientific manipulations, which, it is to be noted, have at least as much power to move us as does the other vision.

What gives these frequent objections their power to move us, sometimes in surprising ways? C. S. Lewis flatly states that the promised power of the new genetics is in fact "the power of earlier generations over later ones." However, since there are no guarantees about their wisdom or lack of it, there is a perfectly understandable fear which stems from recognizing that such power is, as Lewis saw, possessed by some who may or may not allow the rest of us to profit by it. There seems little reason to trust, if not the scientists, then at least those who would have the first and possibly the last word in the use of that power. In a different vein, in an editorial in the issue of *Time* whose cover story was the Hall experiment, Barbara Ehrenreich expressed serious reservations, suggesting that she would agree with Lewis,[108] though her concern takes a different direction: What we should fear is not twenty-first-century technology so much as putting these potent technologies into the hands of twentieth-century capitalists, whose funds, after all, pay the way for these adventures. If not the scientists whose research results in the feared technologies, then the engineers who put the theories to work, and if not them, then those who provide the funding for the enterprise, or possibly those with positions in policy formulation and enactment. Whichever, with the progressive fulfillment of Bacon's vision—in Comte's words, "savoir, pour prevoir, pour pouvoir"—comes as well, ineluctably, a growing sense of mistrust and active distrust.

In a word: We seem strung on the horns of an irascible, perhaps irresolvable dilemma—either to embrace the science of genetics and its apparently invariable companion, the eugenic breeding of people (for which cloning is a key component), or to reject the very idea of genetics, there being no way to prevent a slippery slide from negative to positive eugenics.

Here is the one side: Celebrating genetic knowledge, Eccles and others urge taking control of human evolution, which means, Ehrenreich and Lewis remind us, control by those who have the know-how, and, often, control over the magic of the marketplace to pay for the holy grail of genetics. And the other side: Leon Kass, who decries cloning (and much of the new genetics) as a violation of "the nature of man himself... making himself simply another of the man-made things,"[109] urging strenuous opposition to this "new holy war against human nature,"[110] but this is little more, Weissmann and others aver, than illicit playing on folk superstitions.

Not unexpectedly, of course, the next step down the slippery slope has already been taken, whether Hall's blastomere separation or Wilmut's cloning from adult cells, and the inevitable dispute is again heating up, with Robertson extolling the prospect of cloned children being born "in the next two to five years," and McCormick acidly rejecting the idea that "*anything* that is useful...is ethically acceptable." With subsequent steps seemingly inevitable, is there any way out of these straits?

Is There a Moral to This Tale?

It has seemed to me that what Eccles, Weissmann, Gilbert, and others involved with the Genome Project, tend to forget or pass over, is that, as Jonas urged years ago,

> The biological control of man, especially genetic control, raises ethical questions of a wholly new kind for which neither previous praxis nor previous thought has prepared us. Since no less than the very nature and image of man are at issue, *prudence becomes itself our first ethical duty, and hypothetical reasoning our first responsibility* (emphasis added).[111]

Understandable as it surely is, the rush to find yet another magic bullet, a cure-all promising relief from the loss associated with disease, damage, and other dark things (ultimately, death) about our human condition, is itself cause for serious moral concern. If knowledge is imperative, then, since we simply do not know, or know so little, about our genetic constitution, and even less, it seems, about the very matters because of which genetics seems so glowing—self-identify, intelligence, emotion, playfulness, the gamut of what we do and are—it must surely follow that what Jonas terms "hypothetical reasoning" (perhaps better, the ability of imaginative envisioning or "possibilizing"[112]) is the prime ethical responsibility.

If action is deemed necessary to counteract the devastation of heritable diseases, then surely, since we do not, and perhaps cannot, know in advance what the long-term (and short-term) aftermaths of genetic interventions will be, "prudence itself" is the greater imperative, an ethical responsibility of the first order—to be mindful of what we think and propose to do, of what we risk if we denigrate or think not at all of what, with profound irony, genetics has uniquely forced into question: what, who, how, and why human beings at all are, and whence we go from here.

All things considered, the push for or against cloning may only divert attention from concerns and issues we must face. Considering that most of the reduction in disease and the deathrate were a result less of medicine or science, but instead of better sanitation, sewage, water supply, and other aspects of healthy living conditions, perhaps the best way to ensure that people are healthy is to focus on cleaning up our devastated environment from decades of toxic pollution and radioactive releases. The best way to help people become smarter and more civilized, if not cultured, is not to rely on the fugitive promise of some magic genetic bullet, but to learn to educate far better than we have—a task that must in any event be done. The best way to square off with violence is to help people gain personal self-respect and respect for others, through ensuring decent jobs, housing, and access to needed health and other services. In Barbara Rothman's sharp words, "Our problems lie in darker corners, in poverty and the poor nutrition and inadequate health care and increasing homelessness that accompany poverty in America," not to mention the "costs to our understanding of ourselves as people."[113] For the real problems in our darker corners, there are no quick fixes to substitute for the needed, hard work of thoughtful and imaginative moral reflection, which is, again, a task that must in any event be undertaken, all the more so if those dark corners remain obscure.

Vigorous exploration of our genetic estate is unquestionably important, but only as part of the discipline needed to understand our humanity, our common world, and our future. Too, the talk of rights that has so focused recent social and political discourse has its place in any moral cosmos, but only within a broader, more embracing texture of connections and relations with others. In the end, the fascination with our genetic estate cannot substitute for a clear perception of the all-too-often dismal reality and urgent needs of our moral and social estate.

Notes and References

[1]Earlier lectures were presented at the Center for Ethics, Department of Philosophy, University of Colorado-Boulder, September 17, 1997; and as the Wayne A. R. Leys Lecture, Department of Philosophy, Southern Illinois University, September 28, 1995 (the latter, substantially different, is scheduled for publication in a collection of Leys Lectures).

[2]Ann Geddes Stahlman Professor of Medical Ethics; Director, Center for Clinical and Research Ethics, Vanderbilt University Medical Center.

[3]There is, of course, another, smaller genome initiative nested within the Department of Energy. Its current projects, level of funding,and so on are not clear.

[4]Gilbert, W. (1992) A vision of the grail in *The Code of Code: Scientific and Social Issues in the Human Genome Project*, Kevles, D. J. and Hood, L., eds., Harvard University Press, Cambridge, MA, pp. 83–97.

[5]Surely a winner in any contest would be a recent headline: "Doctors engineer embryos," with the provocative subtitle, "Infertile couples can take 'supermarket approach'" (*The Tennessean*, November 23, 1977, 13A)—announcing what many critics have long feared: "embryos-to-order" reported by physicians at New York City's Columbia-Presbyterian Medical Center, one of whom, Mark Sauer, somewhat carried away by the moment, declared that "it's normal human nature" to want to choose such made-to-order embryos, using a variety of eggs and sperm to make "different pedigrees."

[6]Jonsen, A. R. (1994) Genetic testing, individual rights, and the common good, in *Duties to Others, Theology and Medicine*, vol. 4. Campbell, C. S. and Lustig, B. A., eds., Kluwer, Dordrecht/Boston/London, pp. 279–291.

[7]Ibid., p. 283.

[8]Ibid., p. 284.

[9]Ibid., p. 284.

[10]Identified as the core element in the doctrine of informed consent. *See* Faden, R. and Beauchamp, T. (1986) *A History and Theory of Informed Consent*, Oxford University Press, New York, pp. 277–287.

[11]*See* especially Eccles, J. C. (1970) *Facing Reality*, Heidelberg Science Library, Springer-Verlag, Heidelberg and Berlin, with his numerous references, in particular in chapters I and IV.

[12]Hall, J. L., et al. (1993) Experimental cloning of human polyploid embryos using an artificial zona pellucida, The American Fertility Society with the Canadian Fertility and Andrology Society, Program Supplement, *Abstracts of the Scientific Oral and Poster Sessions*, p. S1.

[13]Shortly after President Clinton convened the National Bioethics Advisory Commission, cloning had clearly become a political football: The American Bioethics Advisory Commission was

organized by the American Life League, Inc., in Stafford, Virginia, evidently anxious that the NABC would not do the right thing—an absolute, unqualifed ban, thus ensuring that already embattled opponents (on abortion and assisted suicide) would continue to be at odds.

[14] Robertson, J. A. (1994) The question of human cloning. *The Hastings Center Report* **24,** 6–14.

[15] McCormick, R. A. (1994) Blastomere separation: some concerns. *The Hastings Center Report* **24,** 14.

[16] Wilmot demonstrated that, contrary to prevailing opinion, a whole mammal could be regenerated from a mature body cell that was specialized for something other than reproduction.

[17] Hall et al. demonstrated that sodium alginate (a seaweed derivative) can substitute for the embryo's membrane, enabling splitting it into undifferentiated cells or blastomeres, with each then placed in different cells and allowed to grow into separate but identical embryos. They 48 blastomeres fertilized from 17 polyspermic embryos, and concluded that the two-cell stage was more likely to develop further than four- or eight-cell stages. But they did not go on to look into that, since it would require unethical use of viable embryos.

[18] Robertson, p. 7.

[19] National Bioethics Advisory Commission (1997) Executive summary. *Cloning Human Beings: Report and Recommendations,* Rockville, MD, p. i.

[20] Reported by various media worldwide, a summary of which is in the American Bioethics Advisory Commission (1997) *Ban Human Cloning*, American Life League, Stafford, VA, pp. 61–64.

[21] Pollack, R. (1993) Cloning humans. *The New York Times,* Nov 17, A15.

[22] To mention several: (1)What if: a pregnancy were achieved and the identical twin embryo had been frozen? The couple later decides their child is so good they want another just like it: the frozen embryo could be thawed, implanted, and, if successful, identical twins of different ages. (2) What if: the first child develops a fatal illness treatable only by transplant; the best chance is to use its identical twin, who would have to be sacrificed in the process? (3) What if: a wife requests she be implanted with the twin embryo her mother-in-law had requested be frozen many years ago; the

mother-in-law agrees, and the wife then presents her husband a gift— his own twin as his son?

[23]For example, as announced Sunday, October 19, 1997, in *The Sunday Times* (London), and sent out over the AP wire: British embryologist Jonathan Slack of Bath University reported he had successfully generated a frog embryo without a head, and then noted that "instead of growing an intact embryo, you could genetically reprogram the embryo to suppress growth in all the parts of the body except the bits you want, plus a heart and blood circulation." Last June, a Japanese scientist announced his success with an artificial womb: Apparently designed for fetuses 20 weeks or more gestational age, his device would, he said, be a positive benefit to women who, for whatever reason, could not carry a fetus beyond that gestational age.

[24]*See*, for instance, Adler, J., Hager, M., and Springen, K. (1993) Clone hype. *Newsweek,* Nov 8, 61; the numerous articles and editorials published in *New Perspectives Q.* **11,** (Winter, 1994). Catholic and Islamic scholars alike condemned cloning as unscrupulous and reverse, and "the arrogance of Western science;" and Kimbrell, A. (1995) "Life for sale." *Utne Reader*, July–August, 26, reporting a patent application from the Centers for Disease Control as the "inventors" of a Guyani woman's cell line. Isidro Acosta, President of the Guyani General Congress is cited as calling CDC's action "fundamentally immoral, contrary to the Guyani view of nature and our place in it."

[25]As Hans Jonas foresaw would inevitably occur; see his insightful argument, "Technology and Responsibility," in Jonas, H. (1974) *Philosophical Essays: From Ancient Creed to Technological Man,* University of Chicago Press, Chicago, p. 18: "...technological power has turned what used and ought to be tentative, perhaps enlightening, plays of speculative reason into competing blueprints for projects...."

[26]Robertson, pp. 7, 9, 14.

[27]National Bioethics Advisory Commission, Session for Friday, March 14, 1997, available from the Eberlin Reporting Service, Silver Spring, MD 20906.

[28]Wolf, S. M. (1997) Ban cloning? Why NBAC is wrong. *Hastings Center Report* **27,** 12–15.

[29]McCormick, p. 14.

[30]Ramsey, P. *The Patient as Person*, New York.

[31]Bayertz, K. (1994) *GenEthics: Technological Intervention in Human Reproduction as a Philosophical Problem*, Cambridge University Press, Cambridge. (Translated by S. L. Kirby, *GenEthik*, Hamburg: Rowohlt Taschenbuch Verlag GmbH, 1987).

[32]Kass, L. (1997) The wisdom of repugnance: why we should ban the cloning of humans. *The New Republic* **17,** (June 2), 17–26.

[33]Jonas, H. (1974) Biological engineering—a preview. in Jonas, H. *Philosophical Essays: From Ancient Creed to Technological Man*, Prentice-Hall, Englewood Cliffs, NJ, pp. 141–167; also Technology and Responsibility: Reflections on the New Tasks of Ethics, pp. 3–20.

[34]Ibid., p. 141.

[35]He undertook this in his last work. Jonas, H. (1984) *The Imperative of Responsibility: In Search of an Ethics for the Technological Age*, University of Chicago Press, Chicago (*Das Prinzip Verantwortung: Versuch einer Ethik für die technologische Zivilisation*, Frankfurt am Main: Insel Verlag, 1979).

[36]Kevles, D. J. Out of Eugenics: The Historical Politics of the Human Genome, in *The Code of Codes*, Kevles and Hood, eds., pp. 9–12.

[37]"Doctors engineer embryos," is the actual headline cited earlier, *The Tennessean*, Sunday, November 23, 1977, p. 13A. from New York's Columbia-Presbyterian Medical Center.

[38]Wolf, p. 13.

[39]*See* Francione, G. L. (1987) Experimentation and the marketplace theory of the First Amendment. *University of Pennsylvania Law Review* **136,** 417–512.

[40]Kass, p. 17.

[41]Callahan, D. (1997) Cloning: the work not done. *Hastings Center Report* **27,** 19.

[42]Childress, J. F. (1997) The challenges of public ethics: reflections on NBAC's report. *Hastings Center Report* **27,** 11.

[43]Zaner, R. M. (1984) A criticism of moral conservatism's view of in vitro fertilization and embryo transfer. *Perspect. Biol. Medi.* **27,** 200–212.

[44]Edwards, R. G. (1974) Fertilization of human eggs in vitro: morals, ethics and the law. *Q. Rev. Biol.* **40,** 3–26; and Kass, L. (1971) Babies by means of in vitro fertilization: unethical experiments on the unborn? *N. Eng. J. Med.* **285,**1174–1179.

[45]The year I came to Vanderbilt—which had started the second IVF program in the United States several months prior to my arrival.

[46]Ramsey, P. (1972) Shall we reproduce? II. Rejoinders and Future Forecast. *JAMA* **220,** 1480–1483.

[47]Tiefel, O. (1979) Human in vitro fertilization: a conservative view. *JAMA* **247,** 3235–3242. *See* my response to Tiefel, "A Criticism of Moral Conservatism's View of In Vitro Fertilization and Embryo Transfer," op. cit.

[48]Goodfield, J. (1977) *Playing God,* Random House, New York.

[49]Weissmann, G. A. (1982) The need to know: utilitarian and esthetic values of biomedical science, in Bondeson, W. B., Engelhardt, H. T., Jr., Spicker, S. F., and White, J., eds., *New Medical Knowledge in the Biomedical Sciences* D. Reidel, Dordrecht, Holland/Boston, p. 108.

[50]Ibid., pp. 109,110.

[51]Ibid., p. 106.

[52]Ibid., p. 106.

[53]Ibid., p. 106.

[54]Ibid., p. 110.

[55]Advisory Committee on Human Radiation Experiments (1996) *Final Report,* Oxford University Press, New York. Of particular interest is the partially dissenting opinion by Jay Katz, pp. 543–548, focused especially on abuses of informed consent.

[56]Beecher, H. K. (1966) Ethics and clinical research," *N. Engl. J. Med.* **74,** 1354–1360.

[57]Pappworth, M. H. (1968) *Human Guinea Pigs: Experimentation on Man*, Beacon Press, Boston.

[58]Jones, J. H. (1987) *Bad Blood: The Tuskegee Syphilis Experiment; a Tragedy of Race and Medicine*, The Free Press, New York.

[59]Engelhardt, H. T., Jr., (1973) The philosophy of medicine: a new endeavor. *Texas Reports Biol. Med.* **31,** 443–452.

[60]Ibid., p. 445.

[61]Engelhardt, H. T., Jr., (1982) Why new technology is more problematic than old technology, in Bondeson, W. B., Engelhardt, H. T., Jr., Spicker, S. F., and White, J., eds., *New Medical Knowledge in the Biomedical Sciences*, D. Reidel, Dordrecht, Holland/Boston, 179–183.

[62]*See*, for example, Bayertz, K. *Genethics*; Annas, G. J. and Elias, S. (1997) *Gene Mapping: Using Law and Ethics as Guides*, Oxford

University Press, New York; Nelson, J. R. (1994) *On the New Frontiers of Genetics and Religion*, William Eerdmans, Grand Rapids, MI; Kevles, D. J. and Hood, L. eds., (1992) *The Code of Codes: Scientific and Social Issues in the Human Genome Project*, op. cit.; Heyd, D. *Genethics: Moral Issues in the Creation of People*; Wingerson, L. (1990) *Mapping Our Genes: The Genome Project and the Future of Medicine,* Dutton, New York.

[63]Eccles, *Facing Reality*.

[64]Eccles, J. (1979) *The Human Mystery* (The Gifford Lectures, 1977–1978), Springer-Verlag Berlin/Heidelberg/New York, p. 120.

[65]*See* sources cited by Bayertz, K.*GenEthics*, pp. 27–37.

[66]Burnett, M. (1978) *Endurance of Life: The Implications of Genetics for Human Life*, Cambridge University Press, London, p. 2.

[67]Clark, K. B. (1973) Psychotechnology and the pathos of power, in Matson, F. W., ed., *Within/Without: Behaviorism and Humanism,* Brooks/Cole, Monterey, CA, pp. 94,95.

[68]Ibid., pp. 96, 98.

[69]Zaner, R. M. (1988) *Ethics and the Clinical Encounter*, Prentice-Hall, Englewood Cliffs, NJ, pp. 199–201.

[70]Toulmin, S. (1990) *Cosmopolis: The Hidden Agenda of Modernity*, The Free Press, New York; and Mumford, L. (1964, 1970) *The Myth of the Machine, Vol. I: Technics and Human Development; Vol. II: The Pentagon of Power*, Harcourt Brace Jovanovich, New York.

[71]Cited in Jonas, H. (1959) The practical uses of theory. *Social Research* **26,** 127,128.

[72]Jonas, H. (1966) The practical uses of theory, in Jonas, H. *The Phenomenon of Life: Toward a Philosophical Biology*, University of Chicago Press, Chicago, pp. 194,195.

[73]As August Comte expressed with great clarity: "savior, pour prevoir, pour pouvoir" (to know, in order to be able to predict, in order to be able to control).

[74]Jonas, p. 205.

[75]Jonas, p. 199.

[76]Ibid.

[77]Tempkin, O., (1973) *Galenism: Rise and Decline of a Medical Philosophy*, Cornel University Press, Ithaca, NY, pp. 40, 85.

[78]Jonas, H. Technology and responsibility: reflections on the new tasks of ethics, in Jonas, H. *Philosophical Essays*, p. 9.

[79]Engelhardt, pp. 451,452.
[80]Jonas, H. *Philosophical Essays*, p. 18.
[81]Ibid., p. 5.
[82]Bayertz, *GenEthics*, p. 23.
[83]Zaner, R. M. (1984) The phenomenon of medicine: of hoaxes and humor, in *The Culture of Biomedicine: Studies in Science and Culture,* Vol. I, Brock, D., ed., University of Delaware Press and Associated University Presses, Newark, DE, pp. 55–69. Also, my *Ethics and the Clinical Encounter*, pp. 199–201.
[84]*See* Edelstein, L. (1967) *Ancient Medicine*, The Johns Hopkins University Press, Baltimore, MD.
[85]Tempkin, O. *Galenism*, p. 85.
[86]Bayertz, K. *Genethics*, pp. 40–46.
[87]Darwin, C. (1974) *The Descent of Man and Selection in Relation to Sex*, revised edition, Rand, McNally, Chicago (reprint of the 1874 edition), pp. 130,131.
[88]Cited in Bayertz, *Genethics*., p. 42.
[89]Ibid., p. 44.
[90]Annas, G. J. and Grodin, M. A. (1992) *The Nazi Doctors and the Nuremberg Code: Human Rights ion Human Experimentation*, Oxford UP, New York.
[91]Ehrenreich, B. (1993) The economics of cloning. *Time* (November 22), p. 86.
[92]Kass, p. 20.
[93]Tiefel, pp. 3235–3242.
[94]Tempkin, p. 40; and Zaner, pp. 199–201.
[95]Batman, G. (1988) *In Vitro Fertilisation in Australia: Discussion Paper and Consultancy Report*, Commonwealth Department of Community Services and Health: Canberra, p. 3; and Collins, J. A. and Milner, R. A. (1991) The effect of treatment on pregnancy among couples with unexplained infertility. *Int. J. Fertility* **36,** 140–152.
[96]St. Clair Stephenson, P. A. (1991) The risks associated with ovulation induction. *Iatrogenics* **1,** 7–16; and Klein, R. and Rowland, R. (1988) Women as test-sites for fertility drugs: clomiphene citrate and hormonal cocktails. *Issues Reproductive Genetic Engineer.* **1,** 251–273.
[97]Whittemore, A. S., Harris, R., Intyre, J., and the Collaborative Ovarian Cancer Group (1992) Characteristics relating to ovarian can-

cer risk: collaborative analysis of 12 U.S. case-control studies. *Am. J. Epidemiol.* **136,** 1184–1203.

[98]Ehrenreich, p. 86.

[99]For instance, Marcel, G. (1952) *Man Against Mass Society*, Henry Regnery, Gateway, Chicago; Ortega y Gasset, J. (1932, 1960) *The Revolt of the Masses*, Norton, New York.

[100]Fowles, J. (1964) *The Agora: A Self-Portrait in Ideas*, Little, Brown, Boston, p. 3.

[101]Ehrenreich, p. 86.

[102]Lewis, C. S. (1968) *The Abolition of Man*, Macmillan, New York, pp. 68,69.

[103]*See* Engel, G. L. (1988) How much longer must medicine's science be bound by a seventeenth century world view?; Schwartz M. A. and Wiggins, O. P. (1988) Scientific and humanisitc medicine: a theory of clinical methods, and Eisenberg, L. (1988) Science in medicine: too much or too little or too limited in scope?, in White, K. L., ed., *The Task of Medicine*, The Henry J. Kaiser Family Foundation, Menlo Park, CA.

[104]Edwards, pp. 3–26; Kass, L. (1971) Babies by means of in vitro fertilization: unethical experiments on the unborn? *N. Engl. J. Med.* **285,** pp. 1174–1179.

[105]Ramsey, P. (1972) Shall we reproduce? II. Rejoinders and Future Forecast. *JAMA* **220,** 1480–1483; Tiefel, H. O. (1982) Human in vitro fertilization: a conservative view. *JAMA* **247,** pp. 3235–3242.

[106]Tiefel, pp. 3240–3242.

[107]Bayertz, p. 65.

[108]Ehrenreich, p. 86.

[109]Kass, L. (1972) New beginnings in life, in *The New Genetics and Future of Man*, Hamilton, M. P., ed., William B. Eerdmans, Grand Rapids, MI, p.54.

[110]Ibid., p. 20.

[111]Jonas, p. 141.

[112]Zaner, R. M. (1981) *The Context of Self*, Ohio University Press, Athens, pp. 165–180.

[113]Rothman, B. (1992) Not all that glitters is gold. *Hastings Center Report* **22(Suppl),** S14.

Abstract

The National Bioethics Advisory Commission's report to President Clinton, *Cloning Human Beings*, lists a number of objections raised by Christian ethicists and moral theologians to the possible application of somatic cell nuclear transfer technologies to human cloning. These objections, summarized under three categories, are generally based on or related to the biblical claim that humans are created in the image of God. It is argued here, however, that these objections are not sustainable.

Objections to human cloning made under "responsible human dominion over nature" fail to tell Christians whether human cloning ought to be regarded as an appropriate expression of the image of God in humans, or as an inappropriate expression of human hubris or pride. Objections made on the basis of "human dignity" fail to tell Christians exactly what it is about cloning that violates human dignity. Finally, those objections made regarding "procreation and families" fail to tell Christians how human cloning will undermine the identity formation of cloned children or the relational and social qualities of family life.

I conclude that the claim that humans are created in the image of God is probably best used to make arguments that humans have moral responsibility and dignity, but that it offers very little in telling Christians how to exercise that responsibility or how to promote human dignity. In the end, then, Christian objections to the application of somatic cell nuclear transfer cloning to humans are probably best viewed as a set of moral intuitions seeking reasons or grounds, rather than as moral arguments as such.

Religiously Based Objections to Human Cloning

Are They Sustainable?

Jan C. Heller

> [A]s technology advances...cloning to produce a child may become reasonably safe.... If so, will that mean there are no lasting objections to cloning?.... If there are lasting objections to cloning, they will be religious.[1] ***Ronald Cole-Turner***

It was only one day after *The Observer* broke the news (on February 23, 1997) that Ian Wilmut and his colleagues at the Roslin Institute were about to announce the successful cloning of a sheep, soon known affectionately to the world as Dolly, that President Clinton sent a note to Dr. Harold Shapiro, head of the National Bioethics Advisory Commission (NBAC). In this note, the president requested that the commission "undertake a thorough review of the legal and ethical issues associated with the use of this [cloning] technology," particularly with respect to its possible use to clone humans, and to report back to him "within ninety days with recommendations on possible federal actions to prevent its abuse."[2] Though researched and written in great haste because of the 90-day limit imposed on the commission, and limited in its comments to one particular type of cloning, known technically as somatic cell nuclear transfer, a report titled *Clon-*

ing Human Beings was in fact completed and submitted to the president in June 1997, with the NBAC's conclusions and recommendations.[3]

In brief, the commission concluded that any attempt to clone humans using somatic cell nuclear transfer technologies is morally unacceptable at this time. Given the present state of cloning technology, this conclusion is based primariy on concerns of safety for the gestational mother and for "the fetus and/or potential child"[4] being cloned. It is thus recommended that the current moratorium on the use of federal funding to attempt to create a child with this technology be continued; that an immediate request be forwarded to all researchers in the private sector, asking them to observe this moratorium voluntarily; that legislation, with a sunset clause included, be enacted to prohibit human cloning; and that any suspension of the moratorium, or any change to the recommended laws, be accompanied by "much more widespread and careful public deliberation."[5]

The report lists a number of other recommendations as well, but of interest here is the commission's consensus that safety is currently the overriding and primary concern when faced with the possibility of cloning a human being. Although few are likely to argue with this consensus, it does, of course, imply—and, in fact, is anticipated in the commission's recommendations noted above—that human cloning could be attempted in the future without undue moral concern, once safety issues are adequately addressed. It is just this implication that worries many religious leaders, theologians, and ethicists. Indeed, the prediction by Cole-Turner in the epigraph of this chapter is probably correct. As he suggests, after issues of safety are addressed, whatever lasting objections are made to human cloning using somatic cell nuclear transfer technologies are likely to be based in religious beliefs. But whether such objections can be sustained is another question. This being the case, I want to assess here the adequacy of these religiously based objections, or, more to the point, the adequacy of the objections made by representatives of the Christian tradition (though I will note, in passing, some of the comments of representatives from other traditions who testified before the commission, or who have written on the subject).[6] First, however, we must determine what we mean by assessing the adequacy of these objections or, as I say in the title of this chapter, their sustainability.

Assessing the Adequacy of Religiously Based Objections

There are a number of ways the adequacy of religiously based moral objections to human cloning might be assessed. First, one could assess the moral objections of any religious person or tradition by evaluating the status or the truth claims of the religious beliefs on which the objections rest. Taking this approach is, no doubt, what leads some secular philosophers and ethicists to dismiss or discount religiously based moral arguments, because they find the bases on which these arguments rest to be implausible.

Second, however, one could ask, with or without regard to the plausibility of the religious bases on which the objections are thought to rest, what implications religiously based moral arguments ought to hold for public policymakers in a pluralistic society and a secular state. This question is raised explicitly in the NBAC's report, and the commission argues that policymakers should indeed make a place for religiously based objections to human cloning, though it is not clear whether they intend for policymakers to treat them as religiously based moral claims as such, or merely as one important source of influence in shaping the interests or preferences of millions of U.S. citizens.[7]

Third, we could assess the objections internally. By this, I mean at least two things. We could assess the objections to human cloning made by religious representatives for their consistency, compared with other similar or related interpretations made by these same representatives or their traditions; or, we could assess them for their ability to consistently guide actions. Like the second approach, the third does not necessarily raise the question of the status of the religious beliefs on which the moral arguments are said to rest (realizing also that what are sometimes offered as religiously based objections may not, on investigation, actually rest on religious beliefs as such). It does, however, ask whether these arguments are persuasive in light of interpretations of other acts or practices supported by the same beliefs.

I will take the third approach in this chapter, though I realize that some readers may view this as side-stepping or begging the hard questions about the status of the religious bases themselves. In defense of my approach, however, it should be noted that if the religious objections fail in this third sense, then they fail all that much more forcefully, since they are not sustainable on their own grounds. Also, my conclusions may have some implications for the other two approaches, because such failure might give secular ethicists greater reason to dismiss or discount religiously based objections and, at the same time, it might also undermine claims that these objections should be taken seriously by public policymakers.

Religiously Based Objections to Human Cloning

The commission's report notes three "major, overlapping themes" that recur in Western religious objections to human cloning: responsible human dominion over nature, human dignity, and procreation and the importance of the family. The report also notes (correctly) that each of these themes can be related to, or inferred from, various interpretations of the first creation myth in Genesis, specifically the claim that humans are created in the image of God. I will review the report's list of the traditional interpretations of the phrase "image of God," and then examine the specific objections developed under each of the three themes mentioned above. I will also suggest that traditional interpretations of the image of God should include reference to the second creation myth in Genesis, namely, the creation of Adam and Eve and their fall from innocence.

The Image of God

The phrase "image of God" is found in Genesis 1:27–28, which is quoted in the commission's report.

> So God created man in his own image, in the image of God he created him, male and female he created them. And God blessed them, and God said to them, "Be fruitful and multiply, and fill the earth and subdue it; and have dominion over the fish of the sea and over the birds of the air and over every living thing that moves upon the earth."[8]

After noting that "[i]nterpretations of the moral meaning of the image of God depend on prior convictions about the nature of God and the characteristics of God that human beings are believed to reflect,"[9] the report goes on to list no less than seven ways in which the phrase has been interpreted in Western religious traditions. Being created in the image of God can mean that

1. human beings are created as moral agents, enjoying the freedom required of moral agency, but also constrained by a corresponding responsibility to God as their creator, to other humans, and finally to the created order generally in how they exercise that agency;
2. humans, since they are created in the image of God, are fundamentally equal, and that their equality transcends all observable differences based on gender, race, class, or ethnicity;
3. humans are relational and social creatures, who realize their personhood and individuality only in community with other humans and the rest of creation;
4. human diversity, though not obviating the fundamental equality of humans, also reflects the image of God and, insofar as God created humans male and female (simulta-

neously blessing and obligating them with the powers of procreation), provides positive warrants for the expression of human sexuality;

5. humans are embodied selves (in contrast to disembodied persons mentioned in Western religious traditions, namely, God and the angels);
6. as embodied selves, humans are both of nature and transcend nature at the same time, and that their creativity, in fulfilling the divine command to fill, subdue, and exercise dominion over the Earth and other living things, is itself an expression of the image of God; and
7. as beings created in the image of God, humans are reminded that they are not, in fact, God or gods, but rather are finite and limited creatures.[10]

One reason to list these seven interpretations here is to show how very malleable the phrase "image of God" is; indeed, a more thorough review of the tradition would reveal that even more interpretations could be listed. One addressed later, and perhaps too briefly in the commission's report, concerns the effects of the fall, detailed in the second creation myth, on the image of God in humans. We will return to this issue below. Here, we need only note that all of these interpretations have been made or developed, with varying degrees of importance and emphasis, in the Christian tradition. Functionally, the phrase symbolizes the way in which Christians (and others) represent the distinctiveness of human beings over against the rest of Creation on the one hand, and, on the other, over against God, as their Creator, and the angels, who are viewed as beings created with moral agency, but without physical bodies. The basic intuition behind these various interpretations is that humans are, at the same time, rooted in the created order, like other living things (being made from and returning to the dust of the Earth), and yet are self-conscious and morally responsible beings, like God and the angels. Substantively, however, the actual content of the phrase tends to change with time and space, at least in emphasis.[11] It should also be evident that some of the above interpretations overlap, contributing nuances of meaning to each other, and that some reveal a certain (some might say, creative) tension between them.

In any case, the ability of the phrase "image of God" to give rise to such a rich array of interpretations is not at all unusual for religious symbols. It is typical of how religious symbols function, especially those that are as fundamental to a given tradition as this one is to the Western traditions of Judaism, Christianity, and Islam. Such symbols are often described as multivalent, a term that suggests how a variety or surplus of meanings can be attached to, or inferred from, the symbol. The surplus of meaning of religious symbols is extremely important to the growth and endurance of religious traditions. For instance, it in part accounts for how a symbol of a given tradition can take on similar, but slightly different, meanings or emphases for adherents in different places and times, permitting the tradition to carry or convey a sense of the symbol's original meanings, and to address the changed circumstances or needs of new adherents.

This said, however, the same surplus that permits religious traditions to adjust and adapt to varying situations, without entirely losing the original meanings of their core symbols, is exactly what makes their moral use so problematic. The problem arises when these symbols are used as moral justifications for or against particular actions, or what ethicists often discuss as action guides, which are not the whole of morality by any means, but they are certainly an important part of it. They typically serve as standards or criteria by which a particular action—in this case, somatic cell nuclear transfer cloning with the intention of producing a human child—may be judged, either prospectively or retrospectively, as right, wrong, or permissible under certain specified conditions. When religious symbols serve, or are made to serve, as action guides, their surplus of meaning often leads to contradictory recommendations for action, or to recommendations that are indeterminate in guiding actions. I will suggest that such is principally the case with the religious objections that have been made to the possibility of cloning humans with somatic cell nuclear transfer.

Responsible Human Dominion Over Nature

One of the principal tensions that emerges from the above-listed interpretations of the image of God concerns the extent to which the exercise of human creativity in the effort to understand and manipulate nature (including, in the case under consideration here, human nature) should be interpreted as an appropriate expression of the image of God, or as an inappropriate expression of human hubris or pride, that is, human usurpation of a role that is properly reserved to God. This tension is particularly evident in interpretations 6 and 7 above, in which the creativity necessary to fulfill the command to subdue and exercise dominion over the Earth and other living things is constrained by the reminder that humans, as created beings themselves, are finite and limited in their abilities. This tension is put into even sharper relief when the second creation story or the fall is referred to in this context.

The second creation myth reminds Christians that humans are not only limited and finite as created beings, but also that they have a propensity to deliberately choose evil, or, at least, to choose in ways that are so self-interested that other humans and other living things are likely to be disregarded or even harmed. In the Christian tradition, the human fall, or fault, is interpreted essentially as an act of overweening pride, that is, an effort by humans to assume a role and perspective that can only be enjoyed by God. However, the Christian tradition also reveals a further tension between those who believe that the image of God was fundamentally affected by the fall, so that, without God's continual intervention (graciousness), humans will always choose evil or in self-interested terms, and those who believe that the image of God was fundamentally unaffected by the fall, so that, humans remain basically good and capable of recognizing and choosing the good.[12] Nevertheless, regardless of how different Christians view the effects of the fall on the image of God in humans, they agree that it is not simply that humans are limited and finite as created beings, but also that they are prone (more or less) to choose evil, or to choose in ways that maximize their individual or their group's self-interest. And it is this tension that, as much as any other, stands behind Christian concerns addressed in NBAC's discussion of the responsible dominion theme, namely, the warnings not to play God, the limits of the human quest for knowledge, the relation of humans to the natural world generally (responsible dominion), and the purposes of human existence (human destiny).

Warnings Not to Play God and the Quest for Knowledge

These two categories can be discussed together, since they intersect so much. Warnings not to play God seem to have at least three overlapping meanings, according to one theologian, Ted Peters, who has written on the subject in the context of genetic research. The first, he says, "has to do with *learning God's awesome secrets*." This meaning addresses the role that the search for new scientific knowledge has in expressing the image of God. The development of the scientific method and new technologies over the last several centuries, especially as these were coupled to the engine of Western economies, have permitted humans to develop powers that are truly godlike. These powers are revealed in the ability to search for and discover new knowledge (pure science), and in the ability to apply it to new and far-reaching technologies (applied science). The possible application of somatic cell nuclear transfer cloning to human reproduction is a case that has called forth warnings about the use of such powers. In this context, the warning not to play God is a warning about investigating certain domains of nature, or about applying what is learned to certain applications, which, in some sense, overstep the limits placed on humans by God. A second meaning refers to the "wielding of *power over life and death*." This warning, claims Peters, is most often leveled against the medical profession, and functions, again, as a caution about human hubris in the exercise of certain types of powers, like somatic cell nuclear transfer. A third meaning, he claims, has perhaps the most far-reaching implications.

This meaning refers to "the use of science to *alter [human] life and influence human evolution*."[13] Although it seems unlikely that somatic cell nuclear transfer, even if it were as safe as any other accepted reproductive technology, would ever be used widely enough to affect human evolution in any dramatic sense, it certainly represents an unprecedented intervention into human reproductive processes. We return to these concerns below. The NBAC's report adds one other nuance to the warning, referring to human inability to foresee or control the outcomes of investigations or interventions into nature, because of our finite and limited abilities.[14]

Responsible Dominion

Under the category of responsible dominion, the report distinguishes three models that interpret the biblical command to "have dominion [lordship] over...every living thing that moves upon the earth" in somewhat different terms. The first model, stewardship, refers to the administrative responsibility of humans for creation, suggesting a metaphor of the gardener. The intuition behind this model is one that expects and permits humans to use and develop nature's resources for their own ends (which is a God-given blessing in Genesis), but to do so in a way that manages and, ideally, sustains those resources for the use of other humans, other nonhuman living creatures, and future generations of both. The second model discussed is partnership. More common in the Jewish and Islamic traditions, though present in the Christian tradition as well, it portrays Creation as an ongoing or incomplete process in which God invites humans to participate, or requires humans to complete, or even to improve. As such, this interpretation may open to more radical types of experimentation with human nature than the first model does, insofar as such efforts could be viewed as an improvement on the original Creation or a creative expression of partnership with God for human good. The third model discusses human dominion in terms of "created co-creators." It moves even further on the continuum toward permitting interventions, though it too is not a carte blanche. Common in some parts of the Protestant tradition, it is counterbalanced by reference to the human propensity to choose evil. As such, a permission to intervene in nature, based in this model, is typically accompanied with a note of caution and a reminder of the need for humility in the face of such powers.

Human Destiny

This category shifts the focus somewhat—though not entirely, because the end is always present in the beginning—from the creation of humans to the purpose of their creation. Again, under this category, the report discusses the extent to which humans are called upon to complete or to improve upon the original Creation, and to participate with God as a co-explorer or co-creator. It may be fair to say that these concerns are less prominent in the Christian tradition than in the Jewish and Islamic traditions. In any case, in those traditions in which it is operative, it may signify somewhat greater confidence (than is present in the Christian tradition, that is) in God's willingness to protect humans from the adverse consequences of their own actions, or, insofar as God created humans to complete or to improve Creation in some sense, a greater willingness to shift the moral responsibility for the adverse consequences of such efforts from humans to God. Finally, though, this category suggests a more permissive stance toward experimenting with, or intervening in, nature's processes.

Now, it is my contention that the arguments developed under these categories, whether taken individually or collectively, ultimately provide little moral guidance to Christians who are trying to decide whether the application of somatic cell nuclear transfer in cloning humans is permissible, forbidden, or obligatory; it seems clearer that Jewish and Islamic interpretations at least provide permission for such interventions. The concerns about playing God or investigating those domains of nature that are off-limits to humans, are simply too indeterminate,which is a point made in the report itself, and by a number of other religious commentators. The problem is that it fails to distinguish for Christians what it is about this particular intervention that should be regarded as forbidden or wrong while other interventions into natural human reproductive processes are regarded as permissible. The three models of responsible dominion present slightly different descriptions of the relationship of humans to the rest of Creation, but seem to function as different ways of asserting that Christians are responsible for their interventions into nature; they do not tell them how to exercise this responsibility, or what criteria to use to help them decide particular cases. The same is largely true about the category of human destiny as well. Most damaging, I think, is the fact that it is not clear—on the basis of the Genesis myths, that is—which of these various models or interpretations should override the others when they conflict. One guideline that does emerge from this discussion might be described as "Proceed, if you do, with caution." However, even this guideline is primarily prudential, does not require the backing of religious symbols, and, of course, does not tell Christians whether or not to proceed. Finally, none of these categories resolves the fundamental tension identified above, namely, whether the application of this technology to humans ought to be regarded as an appropriate expression of the image of God in humans, or as inappropriate expression of human hubris. They provide different ways of conceptualizing the tension, and they offer grounds for some rather sweeping generalizations that seem to follow from these conceptions, but they do not resolve, for Christians, the question of whether the application of somatic cell nuclear transfer to humans is right, wrong, or permissible.

Human Dignity

One way to respond to the surplus of meaning attached to religious symbols, and the indeterminate results when they are used to guide particular actions, is to give the symbols more specificity in moral terms. Discussion of the term as "human dignity" represents one such attempt to specify the meaning of the claim that humans are created in the image of God. This phrase is sometimes further specified by a correlate of the image of God, namely, the sanctity or sacredness of human life. Such specification can give rise, for instance, to moral claims that innocent human beings ought not to be killed, "sacred" here being interpreted as "inviolable." As noted in the commission's report, these categories are prominent in, but not exclusive to, the Roman Catholic tradition.

For Roman Catholics, to be created human, in the image of God, is to possess human dignity. As a result, all human life is regarded as sacred and deserving of respect, with human life having normative status in official Catholic teaching from the "moment of conception" until death. One important implication of these commitments for the discussion of human cloning—one shared, as well, by other Christians, Jews, and Muslims—is that any child born as a result of cloning would be regarded as fully and normatively human, and thus deserving of the respect due to other humans. This means that any child born as a result of somatic cell nuclear transfer technologies ought not to be treated as something less than fully human, as is sometimes imagined in science fiction literature or in the popular press.[15] This said, however, since, in official Catholic teaching, human embryos are thought to deserve the same respect accorded to humans generally, it is argued that they ought not be subjects of research, unless that research can be regarded as therapeutic for the embryos in question. Such could not be claimed for the embryos used in human cloning, to say nothing of those used and discarded in the research required to perfect this technology for humans. Moreover, such embryos could not licitly be produced in any case, since, in official Catholic teaching, the production of human embryos is also constrained by an interpretation of the natural law that permits them to come into existence only through natural means, between a husband and wife.

Taken together, then, official Roman Catholic teaching leads to one of the most consistent positions on the question of human cloning in the Christian tradition. Roman Catholics argue for an absolute prohibition not only on somatic cell nuclear transfer cloning, but also on any reproductive technology that, in their terms, separates the unitive and procreative aspects of human procreation. Such technologies are held to be intrinsically evil, that is, prohibited regardless of the good outcomes they may produce.

Now, although this argument is persuasive to many Roman Catholics, and even to some outside the tradition, the qualifications required to make it requires an interpretation of the natural law (even if we grant there is such a thing) that leads to other prohibitions, for instance, on the use of contraceptives generally, which many find counterintuitive. In the case under consideration here, these qualifications surely stand behind the claim that some Catholics have made concerning somatic cell nuclear transfer, namely, that it would amount to a violation of human dignity. My point is, however, that this claim, by itself, without a consensus on the web of supporting qualifications and interpretations mentioned above, is not persuasive. Nevertheless, when they enter the public forum, some Roman Catholic commentators seem to argue without reference to, or benefit of, these qualifications, and thus their arguments lack the rational support required by the standards of their own tradition.

In the words of these commentators, human cloning is regarded as a violation of dignity, because it would "jeopardize the personal and unique identity of the clone (or clones) as well as the person whose genome was duplicated."[16] Then, anticipating the obvious objection to such a claim, that any clone's genome would be at least as unique as the genomes of naturally occurring twins, these same commentators argue that naturally occurring twins do not represent comparable cases. Twins are said to be different than clones, since the twins are not the "source or maker of the other" as the parent of the clone would be.

But does this argument really address the objection adequately, especially if the clone is regarded by Roman Catholics as being fully human and deserving the same respect any twin would enjoy? Clones are often characterized as delayed twins. Does the fact that one twin is born considerably later in time, or is created from the genetic material of another (which can happen naturally when an embryo splits to produce twins) tell us why cloning as such is a violation of human dignity? I am not persuaded that it does. What is required if such an argument is to be sustained is that we be told exactly what it is about cloning that violates human dignity. It surely is not a violation of human dignity that a clone and his or her parent have identical genomes. This argument would be an example of a crude genetic determinism to which Roman Catholics would not subscribe. In any case, a child cloned through somatic cell nuclear transfer technologies and its parent/sibling would not have identical genomes (such clones would not share the same mitochondria as identical twins would); but even if they did, Roman Catholics would not normally argue that they would not be unique persons. Moreover, the mere fact that clones are born later in time than their twin is surely not enough to substantiate the claim that cloning violates human dignity. The fact that there is greater time between the birth of the twins in cloning than is the case with natural twins does not, on the face of it at least, seem to constitute a violation of human dignity. Some other reasons are required if we are to establish that somatic cell nuclear transfer cloning violates human dignity.

This said, there is a suggestion in the report that what may be motivating at least some of this discussion is a concern for the slippery slope humans may be setting themselves on with such actions. By this, I refer to the concerns expressed for the potential to objectify and commodify the products of cloning; that is, a fear that in their creation, clones will be used as a means to others' ends, or that, once created, clones will be treated by others with less respect than is morally warranted, given their status as human persons. But if this is the concern, it is certainly not unique to cloned children. And, although we might regret that children are brought into the world as products of their parents' self-interested designs, we neither prohibit such children from being conceived or born, nor do we hear arguments that their birth violates (their) human dignity. Moreover, any slippery slope argument depends on actual or highly probable empirical results that may or may not be realized. Arguably, safeguards could be put in place to protect clones from such outcomes, and such safeguards would address the objection.

In essence, then, concerns about objectification and commodification of the reproductive process represent a different type of argument than the claim that cloning is intrinsically wrong because it violates human dignity. What is needed for the latter is greater specificity in the move from the claim that humans have dignity, because they are created in the image of God, to the argument that human cloning violates that dignity. Given the depth and breadth of their moral tradition, such specificity may be available to Roman Catholics, but appeals to human dignity alone are not enough. And, because such specificity for Roman Catholics is constrained by their own understanding of the natural law, it must finally be persuasive on rational grounds alone. More work is thus required if this objection is to be sustained.

Procreation and Families

As mentioned, official Roman Catholic teaching on cloning holds that this technology, and others like it that produce human embryos by artificial means, separates the unitive and the procreative aspects of human sexuality, and that this in itself is an affront not only to the natural law, but also to the dignity of the conjugal union. Other Christians make similar arguments on somewhat different grounds. The Anglican theologian, Oliver O'Donovan, argues that cloning makes children rather than begets them, and that such making diminishes humanity to the extent that it is not natural, or part of God's intentions for human sexuality. The Lutheran theologian, Gilbert Meilaender, also worries that cloned children will be viewed as a manufactured product, and will not welcomed as a gift from God.[17]

But again, other Christians are not persuaded. As the commission's report points out, some do not accept the strong connection Roman Catholics attach to the unitive and procreative aspects of human sexuality, for this connection prohibits (in official Catholic teaching) artificial contraception, which most Christians now accept as morally permitted or, indeed, as obligatory in some cases. Moreover, the distinction between making and begetting may not bear the moral weight O'Donovan wants to give it in this context, because it would seem to rule out other reproductive technologies that are commonly viewed as morally permissible for Anglicans. Also, since Meilaender's argument is a slippery slope argument, whether children born through somatic cell nuclear transfer will be received as a product rather than a gift, as he claims, is an empirical argument that cannot be adequately assessed without some data and, again, a concern that, however regrettably, could be raised about naturally conceived children.

Related concerns about the effects of human cloning extend to the primary community into which children are born, namely, the family. Like a number of other reproductive technologies, cloning permits children to come into families through nonnatural means, raising the possibility that such children might encounter special problems in forming their identities or in forming relationships with other children in the family, who were born naturally. Moreover, unique to cloning, argues Lisa Cahill, a Roman Catholic moral theologian, is the possibility that a child could be born from a single parent. She views this possibility as a "revolution in human history" of such proportions that it should be viewed with "immense caution." Since humans form their identities through networks of kinship, she worries that cloning would result in an "unprecedented rupture in those biological dimensions of embodied humanity which have been most important for social cooperation," since cloned children would not be able to claim "the dual-lineage origin that characterizes every other human being."[18]

Cahill is trying to make good on the claim that cloning in some way violates the natural moral order and is thus a violation of human dignity; that is, she is trying to tell us exactly what is being violated by cloning. This specification is precisely what is needed. But again, we must ask whether her argument can be sustained, because, in fact, a cloned human child would no more relinquish its biological dual-lineage than a naturally occurring twin would relinquish his or her dual-lineage for having been born after the older twin. Certainly, it is the case that the gestational mother of the clone could also be regarded as the clone's twin or sibling, and this unusual relationship might have adverse consequences for the cloned child. But it might not. For instance, if the cloned child is loved and cherished, and perhaps not told of its unusual origins until it is older, it may develop in perfectly normal ways.[19] Thus, although it seems likely that such children would face special challenges, it can be questioned whether the means by which they were conceived and brought into existence would undermine their identity formation to any significant degree. Moreover, although we cannot know for sure, until we have the empirical data with which to work, whether the dire results Cahill fears actually would attend children born through somatic cell nuclear transfer cloning, we can question whether they would be as far-reaching as she predicts, simply on the grounds that cloning is not likely to be a widespread practice. Thus, caution is certainly warranted, but whether Cahill's concerns carry enough weight to justify prohibiting cloning altogether can be doubted. Other Christian ethicists, such as the Protestant, Nancy Duff, are not convinced, either morally or theologically, by Cahill's argument.[20] Neither am I.

Conclusion: Intuitions Seeking Reasons

Some Christian ethicists and moral theologians have raised objections to the moral permissibility of the application of somatic cell nuclear transfer technologies to human cloning. These objections are primarily based in, or inferred from, the biblical claim that humans are created in the image of God. On the basis of this fundamental symbol of the tradition, three major themes were identified in the NBAC's report: responsible human dominion over nature, human dignity, and procreation and families. I have argued here, however, that the objections made under these categories are not finally sustainable.

Objections to human cloning made under the category of responsible human dominion over nature fail to tell Christians whether human cloning ought to be regarded as an appropriate expression of the image of God in humans, or as inappropriate expression of human hubris. Objections made under the category of human dignity fail to tell Christians exactly what it is about cloning humans that violates their dignity. The Roman Catholic tradition probably has the most consistent and defensible objections under this category, provided that one is persuaded by the qualifying and supporting arguments required to make good on them. However, many Christians, and even many Catholics, are not persuaded by these qualifying and supporting arguments. Thus, claims that cloning violates human dignity, because it jeopardizes the unique identity of the clone, are not persuasive. Finally, those objections made under the category of procreation and families fail to tell Christians how human cloning will significantly undermine the identity formation of clones or the relational and social qualities of family life.

To conclude with a cautionary note, however: Even if these objections to cloning fail to persuade, this does not necessarily mean that the Christian tradition is not, or could not be, helpful in guiding adherents on the question of cloning. It does mean that more work must be done by Christians to specify both the meaning and relevance of their objections, and to specify the arguments used in moving from core religious symbols to moral judgments about particular actions. However, it might also mean that Christians ought to abandon the symbol "image of God" as a starting point for moral arguments about particular actions, since it may be simply too malleable to be of practical use in guiding particular actions. In my estimation, the claim that humans are created in the image of God is best used to make arguments that humans have moral agency, responsibility, and dignity, but it offers very little in telling Christians how to exercise that agency or responsibility, or how to realize or promote human dignity. The latter requires a different type of argument. Thus, although this core symbol helps Christians focus the received wisdom of generations of moral reflection on new biomedical technologies, it does little to help them decide whether somatic cell nuclear transfer is right, wrong, or permissible. In the end, then, the objections of Christians to somatic cell nuclear transfer cloning in humans, as outlined in the NBAC's report, are probably best viewed as a set of moral intuitions seeking reasons or grounds.[21]

Notes and References

[1]Cole-Turner, R. (1997) Preface, in *Human Cloning: Religious Responses,* Cole-Turner, R., ed., Westminster John Knox Press, Louisville, KY, pp. xii–xiii. I want to thank Professor Cole-Turner and Westminster John Knox Press for providing a pre-production copy of this book.

[2]A copy of the president's letter is included with the National Bioethics Advisory Commission's report, *Cloning Human Beings: Report and Recommendations of the National Bioethics Advisory Commission* (Rockville, MD: National Bioethics Advisory Commission, June 1997).

[3]Ibid.

[4]There is an interesting question that is not addressed in this chapter of the report on "Religious Perspectives," and it is mentioned only in passing in chapter 4, "Ethical Considerations." It concerns whether it is possible to harm or benefit a potential child either by bringing it or by not bringing it into existence. I will not address this question here, except to say that I argue elsewhere that it

makes sense to be concerned about the quality and quantity of life of such a child, but I do not believe it makes sense to claim that such a child can be harmed or benefited by being brought into existence. This distinction is not merely a semantic one, though it is that too. For example, as discussed below, the distinction would undermine arguments of those Christians who claim cloned children would be wronged by the mere fact of being cloned, since their (alleged) dignity or rights would be violated. I argue that this language makes no sense, and should either be dropped altogether, or replaced with impersonal language that refers only to quality and quantity of life, and not to the harms or benefits certain individuals may or may not experience. *See* Heller, J. C. (1996) *Human Genome Research and the Challenge of Contingent Future Persons,* Creighton University Press, Omaha, and Heller, J. C. (1997) Deciding the timing of children: an ethical challenge only indirectly addressed by the Christian tradition, in *Contingent Future Persons: On the Ethics of Deciding Who Will Live, or Not, in the Future* Fotion, N. and Heller, J. C., eds., Kluwer Academic Publishers, Dordrecht, pp. 71–84.

[5]Ibid., pp. 107–110.

[6]There may be other objections to cloning not addressed in the commission's report that I will not consider here. One that comes to mind is a social justice argument. It goes something like this: as a society, we ought not put our limited resources into such esoteric research until more pressing social needs are met.

[7]Ibid., pp. 92–93.

[8]Genesis 1:27–28, Revised Standard Version.

[9]National Bioethics Advisory Commission, p. 43.

[10]National Bioethics Advisory Commission, pp. 43,44.

[11]Note, for example, the reference to diversity in interpretation 4. This interpretation is not inconsistent with earlier interpretations, but its emphasis is certainly recent. In earlier ages, the fundamental oneness or equality of humans received greater emphasis.

[12]As a generalization, the former interpretation of the fall tends to be found more often in Protestant communities, whereas the latter is more often found in Roman Catholic communities.

[13]Peters, T. (1997) *Playing God? Genetic Determinism and Human Freedom,* Routledge, New York, pp. 10,11. Emphasis in original.

[14]National Bioethics Advisory Commission, p. 45.

[15]This implication does issue in some action guides about how morally to treat cloned humans. Unfortunately, however, it does not tell Christians whether it permissible to clone humans.

[16]Quoted in National Bioethics Advisory Commission, p. 50.

[17]National Bioethics Advisory Commission, p. 52.

[18]Quoted in National Bioethics Advisory Commission, p. 53.

[19]To get some empirical sense of how such children might develop, one could study those families where children are born as a result of IVF or donor gametes, to learn whether the means by which the children are conceived adversely affects their identity formation or the family itself.

[20]National Bioethics Advisory Commission, p. 54.

[21]The author would like to acknowledge the authors of two documents used for background material in this chapter but not referenced specifically. Professor Courtney Campbell (Oregon State University) generously provided a draft of the paper he authored for the NBAC, "Examination of Views of Religious Traditions on the Issue of the Cloning of Humans." I also found Robert Wachbroit's (University of Maryland) short article to be one of the clearest and most helpful I read in my research on the ethics of cloning. *See* Wachbroit, R. (1997) Genetic encores: the ethics of human cloning, *Report from the Institute for Philosophy and Public Policy* **17, no. 4,** 1–7.

Abstract

This chapter first seeks to probe the ethical implications of human cloning from two inclusive contemporary perspectives: American liberalism and its critics. It does not focus on moral principles or conclusions, but on the meaning of human cloning ascribed to, and perceived from, these diverging perspectives of how human existence makes sense. Liberalism and its critics differ on what it means to be an embodied person. Liberalism assesses the human prospect with confidence, its critics with caution. Each appraises the links between individual and community differently, since liberalism centers on the individual; its critics believe that persons emerge only out of supportive communities. Each approaches parenting and the good of children in diverse ways, and they cannot agree in how to talk about all this, since liberals rely on scientific language for referring to human prenatal clones, and critics find such biotechnological terms deceptive, demeaning, and even deadly. Although no one would reject the language of rights, critics regard this concept as too impoverished to do justice to the ethical responsibilities associated with human cloning. A secondary goal seeks to assess human cloning in ways informed by biblical convictions. The results of that effort support the critics of liberalism's world view and of human cloning but fall short of claiming that human cloning is idolatrous. Though the structure of the chapter is one of contrasts between liberalism and its critics, the beginning of promising parallels do emerge.

Human Cloning in Ethical Perspectives

Hans O. Tiefel

The news of the scientific feat of cloning a sheep did not evoke popular press prophecies of flocks of identical sheep (who could tell one sheep from another, anyway?), but of armies of cloned soldiers marching to the orders of a dictator, of cadres of replicated scientific geniuses controlling our future world. To be sure, this was "The Lamb That Roared,"[1] and *Science* magazine honored this achievement as The Breakthrough of the Year. But, for nonscientists, this is not good news, because it forebodes the cloning of the mammal, the one at the apex of all living beings. Although that prospect evokes specters of a brave new world among the public, the birth of septuplets is greeted with sympathetic awe. Such disparity in popular responses is especially worrisome to scientists, who see only scientific progress and yet-undreamed-of biological–medical benefits where laymen suspect a bio-technological menace to humankind. What explains the difference?

The answer may well lie not in a biotechnological marvel that accomplished what was thought impossible, but in a threat to our cultural self-understanding: If contemporary Americans, at least any of college-age, believe anything, they are certain that every human being is unique. And being unique is vitally important, somehow. Although one suspects that such confidence in human uniqueness and its absolute value does not look to fingerprints, DNA, or anything physical, visions of cloned humans threaten with human sameness, and with undermining the dignity of every unique individual.

If that be the logic of popular apprehension, it seems easily refuted by advocates of human cloning, as I shall outline below. But the point here is that the topic of human cloning proves so troublesome and even incendiary to nonscientists, because it touches on our most fundamental convictions of who we are, and of what our descendants might become. The key to understanding this controversy lies not in empirical facts or prospects, but in prior beliefs that give meaning to the facts. Philosophers speak of metaethics here. Believers note fundamental theological implications. Humanists suspect that cloning is an issue about what makes humans human. The intent of this chapter is to set the issue of cloning into the context of the contesting world views of American liberalism and its critics. That task assumes that ethical principles and moral conclusions make sense only when they are seen as emerging from basic convictions about the meaning of human life. Understanding the contestants in this controversy, as probably in all our serious bioethical quarrels, lies in discerning their diverging views of how human existence makes sense. A second goal of this paper is to attempt a response to human cloning that is compatible with biblical convictions and critical of major liberal assumptions.

American Liberalism

Liberalism constitutes a major stream in American culture. Certainly it constitutes the predominant influence in current bioethics. With its roots in the Enlightenment, it branches into all dimensions of our public and private lives. It comprises a major force in constitutional law, forms the parameters of what is reasonable in economics and government, and sets the tone for what is politically correct. Its central focus is the individual person, whose rational and volitional capacity constitute the source of inherent value, and justifies the protective rights of autonomy, privacy, and liberty. Each person counts, not for any religious reason, and not for any contribution one might make to the common good, but because the capacities to think and to decide rationally are our highest goods. I think, therefore I count. Liberalism's great historic contribution has been the liberation of Jews, Blacks, and women. And it continues to champion equal rights of all persons, and fairness in public policy. We hold liberal truths to be self-evident, whether we stand on the right or the left, preferring either property rights or civil rights. We treasure the individual and inborn rights, and suspect that they are perennially threatened by big government, occasionally by big science, but almost never by big business.

Like any living creed, liberalism not only forms visions across the political spectrum, but it also takes diverse patterns, and appears in varying shades of sophistication. The popular anxiety over future countless cloned carbon copies of the likes of us seems to defy that deeply held American belief of individual uniqueness. For how can anything absolutely precious be replicated? To be special, to be ultimately worthwhile, must be something that cannot be copied. Even for objects of art—mere things, and not persons—the value of the original does not transfer to its copies. And if one really could not tell the copy from the original, the worth of the latter would be compromised. Cloned humans appear to have lost the special value that liberalism acknowledges in every person.

But, say the liberal defenders of human cloning, that alarm turns out to be false, tripped by the identical appearance of these imagined look-alikes. Individual identity depends on both genotype and phenotype. Even with the same genetic make-up, different environment and experience will make cloned carbon copies impossible. We do not ascribe identical personhood to identical twins. And even if that great recent maternal feat had produced identical septuplets, we would not worry that their status as future persons was threatened. Individual uniqueness does not depend on genetic uniqueness.[2] More analytically inclined advocates of human cloning can add the reassuring insight that what makes a person unique is not a bodily thing at all, because the person as a thinking and deciding being literally has no looks. It can never be seen, for here "person" is not an empirical concept. The true self is an inner reality and will always remain unique. That should do, to disband the specter of an army of clones being of one heart and mind.

And yet what would be the point of cloning, either animal or human, if we did not wish to create sameness? The chief therapeutic argument for human cloning is to offer the option of genetically related offspring to infertile couples as a new feature of in vitro fertilization (IVF). The cloned offspring would be the genetic duplicate of either father or mother. And if that will not generate an exact copy, at least it will create a spitting image of Mom or Dad—a likeness heretofore discovered with delight, but hardly surprising, and perhaps not universally pleasing in human clones. Indeed, the likeness will be remarkable, because the offspring will also physically be the identical twin of the parent. Although identical twins are not identical persons, "most studies find that MZG twins are surprisingly alike, not just in appearance but in personality and in mental abilities, and that these similarities within pairs...are largely accounted for by genes."[3] Leon Kass similarly questions the denial of sameness by analyzing the liberal insistence of donor consent, when the origin of the nucleus to be inserted into the maternal host is not one of the parents. Why insist on donor consent, when the nucleus is taken from a living body, if the clone will not be the donor in important ways? What harm to the donor, if genotype is "not me"?[4] The topic arises again below, under the rubric of human bodily existence.

Liberalism in its more thoughtful versions inclines to support human cloning. It does so for reasons that emerge from the very heart of the liberal vision: as an affirmation of individual rights, as an expression of hope or confidence in the human prospect, and, as noted above, as an implication of the dualism that separates person from bodily existence. Such liberal endorsement of human cloning finds a natural ally in the language of biological science.

Cloning as a Reproductive Right

Liberalism marches into bioethics battles under the banner of individual rights: autonomy, freedom, choice. One of liberalism's most astute and thoughtful advocates, John A. Robertson, offers a consistent rights-based, procreative liberty approach in his *Children of Choice*. Procreative liberty is a protected activity, because of the importance of reproduction to personal identity and meaning. In almost all instances, "reproductive goals should be respected as a central aspect of people's freedom to define themselves through reproduction."[5] This liberty includes recourse to the broad span of currently available biotechnological options and even future eugenic prospects of enhancing the endowment of offspring. The burden of proof lies on the side of those who wish to prohibit certain practices, such as cloning. Only very profound reasons, such as serious harm to the child, could obstruct reproductive rights.

And yet the child so conceived lacks both moral and legal rights in regard to cloning. Possible harm to the cloned child seems speculative to Robertson, but he also dismisses the moral significance of such harm with a veritable tour de force: If harm results, the cloned person has no ground for complaining, for without cloning he or she would not exist. This is the reasoning courts have used to dismiss wrongful life suits. And Robertson applies this rationale *prospectively*: "The potentially harmful effects of cloning cannot truly harm the clone, because there is no unharmed state, other than non-existence, that could be achieved as a point of comparison.... [E]ven if the clone suffers inordinately from her replica status, there is no alternative for her if she is to live at all."[6] This argument, as the National Advisory Board on Ethics in Reproduction notes, justifies allowing almost any harm to befall children born of cloning, since it can always be said that they are better off alive than never having existed. "It presupposes that children born of cloning are waiting in the void of nonexistence to be summoned into existence and that if they do not receive the call to life, they are harmed."[7]

The more interesting implication of Robertson's individualistic affirmation of progenitors' reproductive rights is that it leaves offspring alarmingly defenseless. To be sure, for most seriously afflicted persons, living a burdened life is better than not living at all. Yet a child could expect its parents to have cared enough to avoid serious risk of harm in bringing it into existence. Robertson does not envision parents being answerable to their child, except with the legal argument: Don't complain; it's either this or nothing! Not only do procreative rights here trump possible harm to the cloned offspring, but such individualism seems devoid of generational solidarity expressed in moral accountability. And Robertson himself seems to have second thoughts, when he concludes that "cloning exerts such a pervasive influence over the new individual that it violates a basic sense of what makes reproduction valuable."[8] A critic notes that Robertson is simply inconsistent at this point, for "if people wish for whatever reason to rear a child who is the replica of an already existing person, there is nothing in Robertson's depiction of reproductive liberty that should lead us to object."[9]

Although, in 1994, Robertson was still dubious about cloning, and insisted that prospective parents would have to use their own DNA or they would not be reproducing, and thus lack reproductive rights, no such doubts exist in 1997. For, "[i]f random, leftover embryo donation for the couple who lack gametes is allowed, a couple should also be able to decide to replicate DNA they know (from a consenting adult not involved in the child rearing), and this should have the same legal protections."[10] Possible harm to the child is dismissed similarly as before: Since the intent is to create life, the procedure must be deemed a benefit to the child, and experimentation would be allowable. The fundamental freedom of married couples to have biological offspring with equal legal protection as other noncoital means has the last word.

Confidence in the Human Prospect

American liberalism as an inclusive philosophy of life offers more general implications for understanding the cloning controversy. Its optimism about the human prospect seems especially relevant for bioethics controversies: Since rationality defines us as humans, it is reasonable to assess the human condition with confidence. Promethean ingenuity, resourcefulness, and courage constitute our most human qualities. Progress is possible, even if it is never without risks. Such faith in human nature endows the future with promise. This winsome quality—I endorse it for its hopefulness of transforming the present into a better future—makes Americans impatient with cynical Europeans, who in turn shake their heads over incurable American naivete. Such confidence in the human prospect has survived two world wars, Vietnam, Freudianism and all similarly depressing psychologies, and is not about to succumb to postmodernism. The liberal version of this confidence makes for an open mind toward new biomedical options, including cloning.

Lest the preceding argument seem too speculative, the godfather of American liberal bioethics leaves no doubt. Joseph Fletcher insists: "It is precisely because men are sapient that they can control their biology. If we like word play it would be better to speak of *homo auto-fabricius*."[11] Fletcher argues that both rationality and morality require control, and entitles his book *The Ethics of Genetic Control*. And that control is the goal of the science of genetics. Against the nay-sayers, he points to hope. And the one hope that unifies all others is "the hope that we will shoulder the responsibility to control quality. The life sciences have made...quality of life the Number One moral imperative of mankind."[12] Animal and human cloning constitute progress toward that imperative, as Fletcher illustrates repeatedly. "Good reasons in general for cloning are that it avoids genetic diseases, bypasses sterility, predetermines an individual's gender and preserves family likenesses. It wastes time to argue over whether we should do it or not; the real moral question is when and why."[13]

Personhood and the Body

Understanding such positive liberal attitudes about biomedical prospects of improving the bodies of our descendants, whether through changing the human germ cell line or through something as comparatively modest as human cloning, expresses beliefs about human nature as Promethean, as requiring control, and as improvable. To use Joseph Fletcher's phrase, we can and should do better than to continue playing genetic roulette by having children the old-fashioned way.

There is also a remarkable reverse side to this confident vision of improving the human body. We need not worry all that much about these ventures going wrong, for this vision of human nature offers a fail-safe quality of sorts: Changing biological features of humans is not likely to affect what makes us essentially who we are, namely, our personhood. For that is not defined in bodily terms at all. A science-fictional android, Data, of television fame, is a person. A human unborn or newborn is not. Personhood, as used in this context, is a mental capacity; it is not essentially tied to human flesh and blood. We therefore need not worry unduly about bodily alterations gone wrong. Unpredictable aberrations seem unlikely to rob us of our personhood. In fact, cloning a cell from a Nobel laureate promises to improve the very quality that makes us what we are: our intelligence. And we also remain prudent enough to monitor our eugenic efforts through quality control that jettisons undesirable abnormalities. In venturing toward an improved humanity, we will lose nothing of importance—a few cells, merely biological human life, detrimental mutations.

Human bodily improvements require prior animal experimentation. We have always improved the bodies of animals, not for their ends, but for ours. The inefficient traditional method, through selective breeding, now yields to more rapid success through such interventions as cloning. And animals may now serve us as never before. Two cloned sheep modified with human genes are expected to produce medicine in their milk—blood clotting protein that can be lifesaving for hemophiliacs.[14] But this is a human project, and the prospect for animals looks grim. The excitement over cloning began with sheep. Dolly is reportedly well taken care of, since its progenitors (its makers?) intend to demonstrate Dolly's unharmed reproductive ability and normal life cycle, because Dolly may not be just a normally maturing sheep since its genetic endowment is eight years older. But Dolly is not like us. Lacking personhood, animals cannot be protected with rights either moral or legal. They are sentient, may feel pain, and may have a good of their own, but we remain their masters. The recent report of the National Bioethics Advisory Commission endorses "humane use of animals" and opposes "unnecessary suffering of animals."[15] That includes using and using up animals, which is a practice as ancient as humans themselves. But liberalism offers no prospect for altering that predatory practice. Biocentric and ecocentric reform proposals abandon liberalism by focusing on features of living beings that humans and animals share. These exclude rationality and volition. If one worries about the morality of animal trials that preceded Dolly, and that now no doubt will grow geometrically, one will find little support in American liberalism. The cloning controversy is really about us, not about dumb animals.

Liberal and Scientific Language

Differing world views, just like different disciplines, require different languages. Everybody speaks English, of course, and no one relinquishes a good word. When liberalism speaks the language of its heart—persons, rights, interests, freedom, dignity—it has nothing in common with the language of science. But liberalism refuses to include human beings in their pre- and nonrational stages within the circle of protectable beings. These earliest of human lives have not yet achieved rational capacities. It is not that they remain minuscule and look nothing like us, but that they do not share our essential humanness of personhood. Here liberalism adopts the nomenclature of the biological sciences. One hesitates to speak of a match made in heaven, but, joined with liberal optimism and support of new biological ventures, this creates a powerful alliance of our major cultural world view and the world of scientific and biotechnological research with early forms of human life. Scientists seeking endorsement for morally problematic investigations are well advised to recommend liberals, secular or religious, to bioethics committees and government ethics advisory boards.

But one cannot do ethics without an ethics-compatible language, and, of course, none of the sciences ventures beyond the empirically descriptive into considerations of value and ethics. To use Roger Shinn's thesis, "science does not prescribe the uses of its powers."[16] Scientific language, to be true to the scientific method, must remain impersonal. And if that language were to become definitive for legal debates, public policy, and bioethics, as it is in the cloning controversy, none of us would have legal, political, or moral standing. If we were all that the sciences can ascribe to us, none of us would have a leg to stand on.

Since the cloning debate is highly technical, the precise language of science seems unavoidable. We are dealing with human products of conception: blastocysts, embryos, fetuses, and clones. Several of these words are backward-looking. "Clone" identifies a life in terms of how it began. Such looking to the past resists the dignifying coloration of words that refer to what it may become, namely, one of us. If we were talking about the cloned human unborn, we might think of them differently.

Indeed the scientific/liberal vocabulary for cloned entities, and for the processes that create them, sound very much like product-language. Here is an ethics advisory board's description of cloning by nuclear transfer:

> [It] involves taking the cell of an animal or human, removing the nucleus, and introducing it into an unfertilized egg from which the nucleus has been removed. The donor nucleus then controls the development of the egg, which, once implanted and brought to term, results in a being genetically identical to the original.[17]

There is, of course, nothing amiss with this language in a scientific context. But these are the words of ethics advisers. This vocabulary becomes definitive, and is used as lingua franca in ethical, legal, and public policy contexts. The cloned entity in the above definition could be a cell culture, or it might be animal or human. This language lends itself to patenting life forms, and to commerce in embryos, and extends all the benefits of animal husbandry to the earliest forms of human lives.

When liberal terminology does offer a nod toward human status as distinct or special, perhaps as a concession to popular and political suspicions, it results in linguistic awkwardness. Here are examples of public concerns: May human cloned embryos be treated just like the embryos of animals? May they be cryopreserved or frozen? May they be created, used, and used up? Federal guidelines generally permit embryo research up to approximately 14 days after fertilization. But even if the law reduces the earliest forms of human lives to research materials, its advocates still feel compelled to profess something more. Thus the guidelines of the ethics committee of the American Fertility Society do not prohibit the creation of a human embryo solely for research purposes. But it also accords the human embryo "special respect,"[18] which, however, falls short of ascribing even the most fundamental right—a claim to life. It may keep human clones from being sold, but one can expect a thriving commerce of animal clones. But this concession seems more an appeasement of popular sentiments than a genuine concern for any dignity of bodily human life. Human clones in their first 14 days of existence may not only become grist for the scientific enterprise legally, as is now possible, but they remain without moral support from American liberalism, as well.

The liberal language for cloning in public debate continues the depersonalizing and dehumanizing nomenclature familiar from the abortion debate, IVF, embryo transfer, and the like. George Annas notes that the uses of "new reproductive technologies have been governed not by the medical ideology of the best interests of patients and their children, but by the market ideology of profit maximization under the guise of 'reproductive liberty'".[19] Annas argues for reform along a medical-professional, rather than a market, model. For human reproductive technologies, he insists that primary consideration should always be given to the welfare and best interests of the potential child. If that is his intent, he may have to stop speaking of reproduction in favor of procreation. He will also have to replace the language of liberalism and of reproductive technology with words that refuse to divorce human lives in their earliest form from the language of care, including medical care, on which we insist for the rest of us.

American Countercurrents

Though American liberalism has formed the mainstream of recent bioethics, it has not lacked critics. Communitarianism self-consciously opposes certain liberal values and policies, but that name itself is a neologism, and liberalism's critics have been around since the beginning of bioethics. Although such counter-currents can be both philosophically secular or religious, the latter predominate. Of course, it can be difficult to recognize religious critics, since most of them assume the liberal maxim that to speak publicly one must eschew religious or particularistic language. And it is no small feat to argue religiously without religious language. Liberalism has become so culturally pervasive that Judaism and Christianity frequently assume liberal guise, but believers who take their bearings from biblical texts will find it difficult to affirm liberal individualism or most of its other core beliefs. To be sure, believers also affirm the starting point of liberalism, i.e., the preciousness of each human being. But that sanctity originates not in rational and volitional capacities, but from an external source. In contrast to the liberal "I think...," believers confess, "We are loved by God, therefore we count." Cloned human beings would, of course, be included in that love, similarly to the liberal insistence that they will be persons with a full panoply of rights, just like the rest of us. Both secular and religious voices will be heard in what follows, as they protest the liberal creed, with religious arguments identified only here and there. Countercurrents emerge out of deep-seated beliefs as well, and include the indispensable importance of community, the affirmation of bodily existence, the search for a language richer than rights, and the reconsideration of parenting and of the good of the child.

The Indispensable Importance of Community

Liberalism starts with and centers upon a fictional atomistic individual, whether in the old-fashioned state of nature or behind a more contemporary veil of ignorance, who may enter promising alliances through voluntary consent, such as a contract. Opposing perspectives, relying on other than Enlightenment sources, note that the emergence of human individuals as persons is possibe only in a supportive human community. Such insistence is not unheard of in the social sciences either. Liberalism looks to the self, and its strengths and its virtues through self-actualization, self-awareness, self-fulfillment, and self-esteem. Dictionary listings of the prefixs "self-" illustrate how much our language and therefore our reality, focuses on the self. By contrast, Western religious traditions ask questions of human identity, not in the first person singular, but in the plural: "Who are we as we make moral decisions about our offspring?"

Liberalism may well have won the day in American culture. Our heroes in film and comic books tend to be superindividuals who do their own thing, even if they accept a partner reluctantly on occasion. It would be odd to hear a heartfelt "Thank you!" from such men (and men always have had an edge here). Their feats may offer some benefit for the common good, but not because society could claim that. Contributions spring from noblesse oblige, or superabundance, or remain mere coincidence. Nor will the Marlboro Man need the community; a good horse and a smoke will do. And if he contracts lung cancer, he will..., well, at least the ideal type will disappear into the woods and die like a man, rather than sue the tobacco company. (Of course, litigation has its own individualistic appeal.) American expressions of humans as essentially social and linked by communal identities and responsibilities are not unheard of, however. Generous responses to regional disasters, and even to famines in foreign lands bespeak a certain national and human solidarity. A national responsibility to the oppressed of the world does not testify to personal generosity as much as to the conviction that we, the USA, stand for something. And if this country were to come under attack, one suspects that volunteers would rush to its defense, quite forgetful of their rights. And, if this listing needs a lighter touch, individualistic Americans prove eager to forget their individual uniqueness in forming the wave, or in claiming "We are number one!" when their only contribution to the team is the price of admission.

Those who decry neglect of community in liberalism not only envision humans as essentially social, but insist that it is important where we come from. That makes traditions important as having sustained those before us, but it also has generational significance. Human cloning, like so many other reproductive innovations, threatens to confound our identities in our begetting and in our being born. In a dissent to the National Advisory Board on Ethics in Reproduction report on human cloning, Thomas E. Elkins, protests that a man and a woman no longer come together to start a new life, and he objects to "continuing to use technology as a means to find ways to reproduce that do not require even human relationships."[20]

To whom we belong and who belongs to us remains important. Yet even before a cloned child is born, its fate literally lies in the hands of strangers. And if its earliest development shows unexpected complications, these strangers must balance their liability against the value of this incipient human life. If it be perfect and allowed to be born, it will not have two parents, but one or several. Contenders include the contributor of the donated cell nucleus, the birth-mother, and the raising mother, as well as the father of the family into which the cloned child is born. It is true that parental love need not depend on biological connections, as adoptions and devotion to the children of divorced and remarried couples attest. I shall return to this point under a different rubric, and merely insist here that knowing to whom we belong and who belongs to us, remains important for who we are, and with whom we share special moral responsibilities. Asexual reproduction confounds our natural familial relationships, and thereby obscures the moral relations tied to them.[21]

An Affirmation of Bodily Existence

Liberalism sees human nature essentially as unique, in that only humans have a mind and will. The ancients may have spoken of humans as rational animals, but the animal or bodily part tends to diminish in significance in liberalism's enthusiasm for human bodily innovation and self-creation. By contrast, anyone affirming Western religious traditions will see the human condition as essentially linked to the earth. In the biblical text, the human, Adam, is of the ground (adamah). Humans are ensouled bodies, embodied souls, and, lest soul invokes medieval echoes of ensoulment, humans are embodied persons, personified bodies. Gilbert Meilaender cites Augustine in describing our existence as terra animata or "animated earth."[22] Though opposing the liberal vision with Christian metaethics, he agrees that we indeed transcend our historical location, but we can only do so as embodied creatures, and our person remains bound to the body, and to its natural trajectory. We begin before we are persons and we may live past our personhood. Our story begins before we are conscious of it, and, for many of us, continues after we have lost consciousness of it.[23]

In such countercurrent, we do not have bodies, we are bodies. And since we are our bodies, our bodies count, either humanistically, because we count, or religiously, because God bestows the divine image on us earthlings and declares this creation good. Then we also are embryonic cells that of late may serve as experimental material for scientifically promising investigations, may be used up within the first 14 days of life for the good of humankind, and may, before long, be produced by cloning. If we are naturally and essentially linked to these embryonic forms of human life—they come from us, we were as they, our children will begin as they—then we may not dismiss them from our community and care. Here the importance of community and the meaning of bodily existence merge: "At issue in debates over human embryo research is a question of membership within our community."[24]

Nor can we remain indifferent to the manipulation and destruction of human lives in their earliest form, without serious implications for our children and ourselves. To dismiss the sanctity of the earliest forms of human beings not only threatens the bodily sanctity we invoke for ourselves, but constitutes a certain forgetfulness about who and what we are. Consequently, we may not take chances with the bodies of our children on the pretext of improving them by cloning, leaving them vulnerable to scientific experimentation and quality control, only to claim them if they survive their prenatal ordeal.

To claim that kinship counts, and that we are bound by blood, identity, loyalty, and care, to those before us, and to those who follow may well offend liberal convictions that ascribe personal value regardless of origin, color, sex, or any other historical accidents. And indeed such bodily links can be absolutized, can dehumanize and lead to genocide. The barbarities of Nazi *Blut und Boden* (blood and soil), and more recent ethnic atrocities, attest to that. Liberalism's devotion to human rights must never go out of style. Moreover, we also can transcend bodily links in adopting, as was mentioned earlier. But, as became so clear in the controversy over IVF some years ago, it is also true that having a child of one's own, of one's own flesh and blood, remains very important to many. The widespread willingness to go to the trouble and expense of conceiving by IVF confirms such importance. One hesitates to invoke nature over against culture here. In any case, appreciating and grounding moral responsibility in bodily links with children and other kin is ancient. Even the first man rejoiced over his offspring: "This at last is bone of my bones and flesh of my flesh" (Genesis 2:23). One trusts that Eve's personhood was also important to Adam, since the story includes shared rational and volitional (and disastrous) decisions.

The Search for a Language Richer than Rights

Liberalism tends to affirm human cloning as an expression of rights, or to be exact, of reproductive liberty.[25] But rights are difficult to apply to future generations, as attempts to develop a liberal approach to ecological ethics shows. Rights are claims, and who is to advocate the rights of those to come, who literally have no standing, against us who are moral and legal rights-holders beyond doubt? Although rights remain indispensable protections for when we fail each other, they prove inadequate for expressing and affirming our responsibilities to our children (or to each other). We insist on a right to child support, but how shameful for any neglectful parent that it should come to that. Rights are individualistic, adversarial, and defensive. Family solidarity and devoted care should pre-empt the need for rights. It should never come to that.

Actually, that holds true, ironically, for the liberal understanding of rights in the case of a cloned offspring—it never comes to that. For the human unborn have no legal rights under our liberal laws of the land, and lack ethical rights, as well, in the liberal cosmos. Once the child becomes a person, more or less, it does acquire ethical rights. But by then the imposition of cloning and its risks and consequences prove irreversible. Then it is too late, as John Robertson explained.

But if they had even negative rights, rights that ward off intrusions, from what might candidates for cloning be protected?

Or from what might devoted parental care shield these potential cloned offspring? Most immediately, of course, they should be protected from the fatal liberal vision that reduces them to research material, that subsumes them completely under the reproductive rights of their progenitors, that affirms the dignity of cloned persons, but recommends running them through technological gauntlets before they reach personhood. Cloning has elicited widespread warnings against dehumanizing clones. But they, and therefore we, have more to fear from the narrow vision of liberalism itself. It is not the specter of cloned humans that should frighten us, as much as what the readiness to clone humans says about us.

Rights ordinarily protect our children from harm. But American unborn children have no rights, and will not be protected from experimental risks, even when a cloned child is wanted. The successful British team transferred 277 adult nuclei into enucleated sheep ova, implanted 29 resulting embryos, and celebrated the singular Dolly. Parental care, observing a minimum of foresight, might be reluctant to place a child-to-be into the hands of experts who face such or worse odds of success. Of course, the odds will improve in time. Once these pediatric pioneers have paid the price, and statistics come close to natural embryonic loss, the cost of human sacrifice to scientific progress and human projects may seem reasonable.

Reconsideration of Parenting and of the Good of the Child

Protection from us, then, is what parental anticipative fidelity might counsel. Not just from us when we formulate liberal public policy for human cloning but from us as parents. One hesitates to use the word "parent," since its designation now may include the nucleus donor, and limits genetic parents to one. But parent it shall be here, to create some basis on which to establish responsibility for the child-to-be. Liberalism would widen or expand our concept of parenting, ascribing remarkable new meaning to the single-parent child. Antagonists dismayed by such linguistic liberty insist on remembering and reconsidering what it means and should mean, to become and be a parent.

Some critics base their objection to human cloning on the parental responsibility not to harm the child, and to seek its good. They assert that cloning may or will harm the child, and will not benefit it. Such conclusions seem premature. Critics of human cloning should grant that this innovation, apart from the risks of experimental procedures, need not harm the child, and may in fact benefit it. Choosing only the best donor-nucleus, however we define "best," promises to give advantage to the child. Moreover, cloning avoids genetic roulette, to use Joseph Fletcher's catchy phrase. And sharing another human's genotype, as with a twin, implies no offense, and may gratify. But that does not answer the questions of whether such benefit outweighs the risks, and whether offering such benefit is fair.

To consider the last question first, asking if it is fair to give advantage to a cloned child genetically, is deontological and focuses on means (though not the means of how to pay for it). May a parent fairly seek such advantage? Will the majority be subject to unfairness through the superior endowment of what will foreseeably remain a small minority? The question may resemble the current debate over affirmative action. Enriching this child with the best genetic endowment does give it an inborn advantage over others who remain children unimproved. This advantage remains unearned and insuperable. Americans may aspire to be self-made men (and women), but this self-making is beyond the reach of anyone who is not born with it. Our sense of justice insists on a level playing field and seeks to redress inherited disadvantages. But the playing field, on which superior cloned children compete will always remain tilted. To be sure, the world was always unfair. And some parents could give their children a better boost in life than others. The answer, then, is that offering this benefit is unfair, and that we should not add to the world's unfairness.

But is a superior genetic endowment not a novel and very special gift that a parent might give the child? Though counterfactuals may omit some vital feature of reality, imagine that we eliminated the time gap and gave the prospective cloned child a mature voice in this issue. Of course none of us has a choice to be born. Nature is not that liberal. But suppose that the prospective child were offered the choice of a magnificent genetic gift. The parent offers this superior endowment: "Take it, it's good for you." And the child might then accept or refuse, already using its own judgment of what is good. Gifts are offers to which recipients must respond. This may be an offer too good to refuse, but even the best offer offers a choice. Indeed, even God's gifts seem to face that limit, given insistence on the free response of covenant partners. But of course that is precisely what cannot happen in actual parental decisions to clone: The child cannot accept this offer intended as a gift. And what is given can never subsequently be refused. Therefore even if cloning results in the good of the child, it cannot constitute a gift.

But return to the question of whether cloning is good, on balance, for the child. This question must be asked by parents, by prospective parents, and by our society. Cloning might bestow advantages on the child, but will it be for good, on balance? The discussion over cloning actually offers few reflections on that question. Hardly anyone neglects to consider harm to the cloned child. And the National Bioethics Advisory Committee made risk of harm its central argument in concluding that, at this time, it is morally unacceptable for anyone to attempt to create a child using somatic cell nuclear transfer cloning. Considerations of possible harm to the dignity of a cloned child also seem ubiquitous, usually with the result of being easily dismissed. But absence of harm does not answer the question of whether cloning is good for children. It may be good for progenitors.[26] If arguments exist that cloning would be good for cloned children, I have missed them. The lone voice that counsels attention to the needs of children is that of Daniel Callahan:

> Nowhere has anyone suggested that cloning would advance the cause of children.... [I]t has been one of the enduring

> failures of the reproductive rights movement that it has, in the pursuit of parental discretion and relief of infertility, constantly dissociated the needs of children and the desires of would-be parents.[27]

Again, is it good for the child? This looks like the sort of question on which social scientists might shed light. Sociological and psychological emphasis on relationships appears to be less than supportive of individualistic procreative liberty to clone.

> While the internalized psychological image of a family and the intention to belong to a family are part of the foundations of a family, there is no denying the bond created by genetic kinship.... [H]aving both sets [of lineages] provides important social resources. The child is heir to more than money or property when situated in a rooted kinship community.... Psychology has come to see genetic factors as more and more important in parent–child interactions and childrearing outcomes.[28]

Cloning promises prospective parents unparalleled power. Obversely, it exposes children to new vulnerability. New human life has always been placed into human hands. One could reply that such exposure constitutes the human condition. And, indeed, anyone with a sense of community acknowledges that we are all placed into each other's hands (the nuclear code briefcase ever at the president's hand is only its most startling expression.) Children have always been in the hands of their parents, for better or worse. But now parental hands hold so much more power. We cannot only call a human being into life, but can determine its genetic identity. Children have always had to take what they get. But cloning leaves children defenseless against the bodily choice we make for them. True, they remain defenseless in so many other situations, since not all begetting has been responsible (as in knowingly conceiving as a carrier of serious genetic disease or of AIDS). Yet such wrongs do not make a right. Here the relations and identities between progenitor and offspring change drastically. "I made you into what you are" has never been so true. And never have parents been such masters. Some will want to choose this role. No one should, especially not the ones who would so choose. Loving one's children means to serve them, not to lord it over them.

Animal and plant cloning are instrumental. Cloning will produce some benefit for the cloner. If that beneficent logic transfers to humans, all but utilitarian teeth will be set on edge. All but the most consistent consequentialists might find the Kantian protest telling: We must not use persons merely as means to our ends. Is this the logic of human cloning? We do say that we have children and that they are ours. But when parents do make their children serve their needs, their ambitions, and their projects, we suspect that they fall short of getting it right. We do expect that our children will make our lives better, but that expectation probably does not survive the first night that the newborn comes home. One might argue that expectations that children should serve their parents expressed family loyalty and honored parents. But parental roles in bringing children into the world must be one-way, directed to the good of the child. To decide to make one's children after one's own image, or an image of one's choosing, is despotic.[29] It will also probably be hard on the kid to live up to the qualities that made his genetic predecessor imitable. But that must not be the last word. Ted Peters is right when he claims that "[s]elf-fulfillment for parents and dignity for children are not necessarily competitors; they can be complementary."[30] If that is true in the context of human cloning, then that choice may be, but need not be, instrumental.

Is the choice to clone compatible with being a good parent? Maybe the prospect of eventually having to justify this choice to one's cloned child holds part of the answer. Unless one intends to be a lawyer toward one's children, would one really want to face one's child knowing oneself to be responsible for what it is—what it is that we see, hold, touch, embrace? Do we threaten the dignity of our children in such reproduction, through our control over them, even as we give them life? Another partial answer may depend on one's view of human nature. Certainly biblical traditions do not evoke liberal optimism about the human prospect. Rather, they elicit a sense of realism that all of us, like our first parents, find it tempting "to be like God" (Genesis 3:5), with less than optimal results.

Neglected Themes

The debate over human cloning ranges so widely that relatively few arguments could be pursued in depth here. Offering at least pointers toward some themes neglected in this chapter may not shed much light, but it will indicate how limited this chapter has been. Pursuing parallels between liberalism and its critics might be particularly promising. An additional word about animal cloning from religious perspectives would balance its earlier mention.

Promising Parallels

Juxtaposing liberalism and its critics makes sense insofar as they do differ in their assessment of the human condition, of how to talk about it, and of human cloning. That structure obscures possible agreements between them, however. Yet the point about consent to cloning as a gift to the cloned child might appeal to both perspectives. And the argument about a level playing field would be liberally kosher.

Karen Lebacqz, with credentials in both liberal and Christian contexts, offers a third congruence, with an eloquent argument that merits quoting in full:

> In a world that groans under the weight of injustice, in a world in which children die of malnutrition by the thousands every day, in a world in which children's growth is stunted by chronic hunger, is there not something wrong with the question for ever more and more exotic technologies to privilege the already privileged?[31]

Why should it be so important to clone either our own or someone else's genetic identity? Human cloning will not constitute a new therapy; it does not heal anyone. If it addresses human suffering, it is a distress that might be relieved by such alternatives as adoption. To recognize that having a child of one's own is rightly important to many does not preclude a nongenetic, ethical, and religious redefinition of this expression. Nor does this distressing need rank it near the top of medical and biotechnological priorities for relieving the human estate.

The Status of Animals Among Religious Critics of Liberalism

If truth be told, religious writers have more to say than liberals about protecting animals in the context of cloning, but animals may well fear them both. Although religious authors omit any implied denigration of animals as mere bodily beings, animals—wistfully, to be sure—may still be used and used up. Only the likes of us are created in the image of God. And though God is the Creator of animals, and cares for them, too, that cuts little ice. One looks in vain for a Francis of Assisi among religious writers in the context of the cloning debate, though two authors do claim that, for both animals and humans, "the ultimate purpose...is nothing less than to praise God."[32] That leaves penultimate purposes. One finds objections to cruelty without awareness that whatever is done to animals will never be so named by those who "make carefully controlled use of animals" in experiments "undertaken for serious and beneficial ends." Although respect is in order, the ethical logic is instrumental, and the biblical text is that of dominion (Genesis 1:26). Vegetarianism is not a recognized Christian virtue. And objecting to animal experimentation does smack of antiscience conservatism. Much work remains to be done here, probably in connection with ecological ethics.

Other Neglected Themes

This chapter has evaded questions about what is natural or unnatural, because these concepts are so hard to pin down, and are difficult to distinguish from what is traditional-cultural or from what is artificial. Besides, "the mastery of nature through technological problem solving is also completely natural to us—indeed, it is the glory of *homo sapiens*."[33] The role of scientists in the debate over the ethics of cloning remains untouched, but surely they owe us more than helping lay folk get the facts straight. Probing the implications of cloning for women, as distinct from men, would keep the reader alert, because women, in contrast to men, prove indispensable here, and can play even more maternal roles than in IVF. Cloning's link with eugenics was only adverbially mentioned. This chapter almost wholly omits the background of the cloning controversy 30 years ago. Cryopreservation of human clones, producing clones for organ donations, using up one clone to test the quality of another, the relevance of cloning to medical care—the list goes on. Important arguments remain unresolved or ignored.

Summary and Conclusions

This chapter has probed the ethical implications of human cloning from two inclusive contemporary perspectives: American liberalism and its critics. It has not focused on moral principles or conclusions, but on the meaning of human cloning ascribed to, and perceived from, these diverging perspectives of how human existence makes sense. Liberalism and its critics differ on what it means to be an embodied person. Liberalism assesses the human prospect with confidence, its critics perceive it with caution. Both appraise the links between individual and community differently since liberalism centers on the individual, and its critics believe that persons emerge only out of supportive communities. Both approach parenting in diverse ways. And they cannot agree in how to talk about all this, since liberals rely on scientific language for referring to human prenatal clones, and critics find such biotechnological terms deceptive, demeaning, and even deadly. Although no one would reject the language of rights, critics regard this concept as too impoverished to do justice to the ethical responsibilities associated with human cloning. A secondary goal has been to assess human cloning in ways informed by, or at least compatible with, biblical convictions. The result of that effort supports the critics of liberalism's world view and of human cloning, but falls short of claiming that human cloning is idolatrous.[34] Though the structure of the chapter is one of contrasts between liberalism and its critics, the chapter describes at least the beginning of promising parallels.

Those who consider human identity to be inconceivable apart from bodily existence cannot live with the liberal person–body dualism, simply because, for many among us, there is no living with it. If only our mind really counts, counts enough to demand dignity and respect, the implications for human beings across the life span—not only for us as the cloned unborn, but for us in our aging senility, or in our mental retardation—prove savage and lethal. But these are the very humans, the least among us, who the God of Israel and of the Christian Church deems so dear as to identify with them (Matthew 25:31–46). Ironically, clonally reproducing a human being actually overvalues the intended body and the personal qualities it promises, because our worth and standing arise not from within, but from our relationships with those who love us. Therefore, there should be no human cloning and no research with cloned human embryos. But if children will be cloned, they will be welcomed into our community of care. And they will need a special welcome, since they have survived the manipulation of their creators, and live under the shadow of meeting the expectations of the image in which they were produced.

Notes and References

[1]Pennisi, E. (1997) The lamb that roared. *Science*, **278,** 2038.

[2]Macklin, R. (1994) Splitting embryos on the slippery slope: ethics and public policy. *Kennedy Inst. Ethics J.* **4,** 215–218.

[3]Cole-Turner, R. (1997) At the beginning, in *Human Cloning: Religious Responses*, Cole-Turner, R., ed., Westminster John Knox Press, Louisville, KY, p. 123.

[4]Kass, L. R. (1997) The wisdom of repugnance. *The New Republic,* June 2, 23.

[5]Robertson, J. A. *Children of Choice: Freedom and the New Reproductive Technologies*, Princeton University Press, Princeton, NJ, p. 18. For those who oppose human cloning, law professor Robertson has become an indispensable focus.

[6]Robertson, *Children of Choice*, p. 169.

[7]National Advisory Board on Ethics in Reproduction (1994) Report on human cloning through embryo splitting: an amber light. *Kennedy Inst. Ethics J.* **4,** 258. Although cloning here refers to embryo splitting, the point applies to cloning defined as nuclear transplantation as well.

[8]Ibid.

[9]Meilaender, G. C. (1995) *Body, Soul, and Bioethics,* University of Notre Dame Press, Notre Dame and London, p. 67.

[10]Pollner, F. (1997) The ethics of cloning: a model of heterogeneity. *The_NIH Catalyst* p. 7.

[11]Fletcher, J. (1974) *The Ethics of Genetic Control: Ending Reproductive Roulette,* Anchor Press/Doubleday, Garden City, NY, p. 4.

[12]Ibid., p. 196.

[13]Ibid., p. 154.

[14]Weiss, R. (1997) 2 New clones carry human clotting gene. *The Washington Post*, December 19, A27, A29.

[15]National Bioethics Advisory Commission (1997) *Cloning Human Beings: Report and Recommendations,* Rockville, MD, pp. iv and 79. Of course, this report addresses human, not animal, cloning.

[16]Shinn, R. L. (1997) Between eden and babel. *Human Cloning*, Cole-Turner, R., ed., Westminster John Knox, Louisville, KY, p. 107.

[17]National Advisory Board on Ethics in Reproduction (1994) 251,252.

[18]National Advisory Board on Ethics in Reproduction, 263.

[19]Annas, G. J. (1994) Regulatory models for human embryo cloning: the free market, professional guidelines, and government restrictions. *Kennedy Inst. Ethics J.* **4,** 235.

[20]National Advisory Board on Ethics in Reproduction, 282.

[21]Kass, 21.

[22]Meilaender, pp. 38 and 49.

[23]Ibid., p. 59.

[24]Ibid., p. 99.

[25]Kass outlines the possible meanings of reproductive rights for those considering having a cloned child, (Kass, 24). My focus is on what rights might mean for the cloned.

[26]The National Bioethics Advisory Commission describes possible progenitor advantages on page 80 of its report on cloning.

[27]Callahan, D. (1997) Cloning: the work not done. *Hastings Center Report* **27,** 19.

[28]Callahan, S. (1988) The ethical challenge of the new reproductive technology, in *Medical Ethics: A Guide for Health Professionals*, Monagle, J. F. and Thomasma, D. C., eds., Aspen Publishers, Rockville, MD, p. 31.

[29]Kass, 24.

[30]Peters, T. (1997) Cloning shock: a theological reaction, in *Human Cloning*, Cole-Turner, R., ed., Westminster John Knox, Louisville, KY, p. 22.

[31]Lebacqz, K. (1997) Genes, justice, and clones, in *Human Cloning*, Cole-Turner, R., ed., Westminster John Knox, Louisville, KY, pp. 54,55.

[32]Hauerwas, S. and Shuman, J., (1997) Cloning the human body, in *Human Cloning*, Cole-Turner, R., ed., Westminster John Knox, Louisville, KY, p. 65.

[33]Callahan, S., p. 27.

[34]Hauerwas and Shuman, p. 65.

Bibliography

Annas, G. J. (1994) Regulatory models for human embryo cloning: the free market, professional guidelines, and government restrictions. *Kennedy Inst. Ethics J.* **4,** 235–249.

Callahan, D. (1997) Cloning: the work not done. *Hastings Center Report* **27,** 18–20.

Cole-Turner, R. (1997) At the beginning, in *Human Cloning: Religious Responses*, Cole-Turner, R., ed., Westminster John Knox, Louisville, KY, pp. 119–130.

Fletcher, J. (1974) *The Ethics of Genetic Control: Ending Reproductive Roulette*, Anchor Press/Doubleday, Garden City, NY.

Hauerwas, S. and Shuman, J. (1997) Cloning the human body, in *Human Cloning*, Cole-Turner, R., ed., Westminster John Knox, Louisville, KY, pp. 58–65.

Kass, L. R. (1997) The wisdom of repugnance. *The New Republic*, June 2, 17–26.

Lebacqz, K. (1997) Genes, justice, and clones, in *Human Cloning*, Cole-Turner, R., ed., Westminster John Knox, Louisville, KY, pp. 49–57.

Macklin, R. (1994) Splitting embryos on the slippery slope: ethics and public policy. *Kennedy Inst. Ethics J.* **4,** 209–225.

Meilaender, G. C. (1995) *Body, Soul, and Bioethics*, University of Notre Dame Press, Notre Dame and London.

National Advisory Board on Ethics in Reproduction (1994) Report on human cloning through embryo splitting: an amber light. *Kennedy Inst. Ethics. J.* **4,** 251–282.

National Bioethics Advisory Commission (1997) *Cloning Human Beings: Report and Recommendations,* Rockville, MD.

Pennisi, E. (1997) The lamb that roared. *Science* **278,** 2038,2039.

Peters, T. (1997) Cloning shock: a theological reaction, in *Human Cloning*, Cole-Turner, R., ed., Westminster John Knox, Louisville, KY, pp. 12–24.

Pollner, F. (1997) The ethics of cloning: a model of heterogeneity. *The NIH Catalyst*, May–June, 6–8.

Robertson, J. A. (1994) *Children of Choice: Freedom and the New Reproductive Technologies,* Princeton University Press, Princeton, NJ.

Shinn, R. L. (1997) Between eden and babel, in *Human Cloning*, Cole-Turner, R., ed., Westminster John Knox, Louisville, KY, pp. 106–118.

Weiss, R. (1997) 2 New clones carry human clotting gene. *The Washington Post*, December 19, A27, A29.

Index

G

H

I